SEVEN YEARS
of
Highly
Defective
People

Scott Adams' Guided Tour of the Evolution of **DILBERT**

BY SCOTT ADAMS

Andrews McMeel
Publishing

Kansas City

Other DILBERT Books from Andrews McMeel Publishing

Casual Day Has Gone Too Far
Fugitive from the Cubicle Police
Still Pumped from Using the Mouse
It's Obvious You Won't Survive by Your Wits Alone
Bring Me the Head of Willy the Mailboy!
Shave the Whales
Dogbert's Clues for the Clueless
Build a Better Life by Stealing Office Supplies
Always Postpone Meetings with Time-Wasting Morons

For ordering information, call 1-800-642-6480.

DILBERT® is a registered trademark of United Feature Syndicate, Inc.

DOGBERT and DILBERT appear in the comic strip DILBERT®, distributed by United Feature Syndicate, Inc.

http://www.unitedmedia.com/comics/dilbert

www.andrewsmcmeel.com

ISBN: 0-8362-5129-6 hardback
       0-8362-3668-8 paperback

Library of Congress Catalog Card Number: 97-72286

To subscribe to the **Dilbert** newsletter, send e-mail to
listserv@listserv.unitedmedia.com in the following format:
        subject: newsletter
        message: Subscribe Dilbert_News Firstname Lastname

Don't include any other information—your e-mail address will
be picked up automatically.

If the automatic method doesn't work for you, you can
also subscribe by writing to scottadams@aol.com or via
snail mail:

        Dilbert Mailing List
        c/o United Media
        200 Madison Avenue
        New York, NY 10016

ATTENTION: SCHOOLS AND BUSINESSES

Andrews McMeel books are available at quantity discounts with bulk purchase
for educational, business, or sales promotional use. For information, write to:
Special Sales Department, Andrews McMeel Publishing, 4520 Main Street,
Kansas City, Missouri 64111.

Yeah, yeah it's for Pam.

Contents

● **Introduction** 7

● **Dilbert** 8
... at Home with Dogbert .11
... and Technology 17
... in the Business World 27
... and Women 62
... and His Ego 70
... Dies 72
... Travels 74
... Attempts to Join the Consumer Society 75

● **Dogbert** 80
... the Early, Vulnerable Days 82
... Reveals His Sarcasm 92
... the Many Occupations 100
... Schemes to Conquer the World 111
... Saving Dilbert 125

● **Ratbert** 128

● **Garbageman** 138

● **Liz** 142

● **Mom and Dad** 150

● **Bob the Dinosaur** 154

● **Catbert** 162

● **Phil** 168

● Asok 174

● Tina the Tech Writer 178

● Elbonians 184

● The Boss 188

● Alice 208

● Wally 216
   . . . and Hygiene Issues .224

● Carol 226

● Critters 230

● Dogbert in Hats 240

● Ted the Generic Guy 244

● Slapstick 250

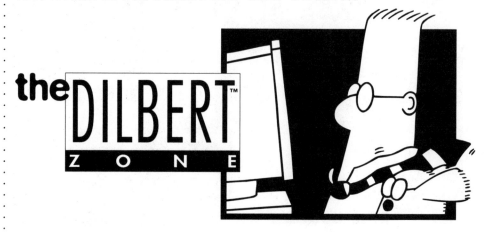

Introduction

You'll see a bunch of semi-legible, handwritten notes in the margins of this book. Those are mine. It's best to read each cartoon first and then the related note. Some of the notes are fascinating insights into the world of cartooning. Other notes are interesting only for their poor grammar and spelling, thus proving that you can be a moron and still have a successful career as a cartoonist. Either way, it's inspirational.

I made all of the notes in three sittings. I stopped only long enough to rest my weary hand. The thoughts are off the top of my head — which I can prove — because there's a little bald spot where the thoughts took off.

My hand is weary. That means the introduction is done.

Scott Adams

I was heavily into puns in the early days.

Dilbert was a doodle long before he had a name. He was a composite of my co-workers at Crocker Bank and later Pacific Bell. I worked with a lot of technical people and noticed that many of them had potato-shaped bodies and glasses. When I morphed them together in my brain they became Dilbert. I suppose I doodled the technical people more than other people because they seemed more interesting to me, both in personality and in appearance.

I'm often asked why Dilbert has no mouth and why his necktie curls up. The truth is that I don't know. The best answer I can give is that "it looks right." As a doodle, he was never drawn exactly the same. There were times in his doodle-days when he had a mouth and a flat tie. His body and head shape have changed gradually. He even had visible eyes once. In time I developed a preference for what "looked right" with him. It would be easy to interpret his lack of mouth and his uncontrolled necktie as symbols of his powerlessness, but I can't claim to be that clever. All I know is that I like him drawn that way.

I drew the little pre-Dilbert character to add interest to my own presentations at work. Sometimes I'd draw rebellious cartoons on the whiteboard of my cubicle for the amusement of my co-workers. People started wondering what his name was. It seemed appropriate to give him one. So I had a "Name the Nerd" contest on my whiteboard and invited people to write their suggestions below his picture.

Several people wrote in their suggestions, but none of them seemed right. Then a truly strange thing happened. My friend

Mike Goodwin stopped by to tell me he had the name. He picked up the erasable marker and wrote "Dilbert."

I ended the contest immediately and declared Mike the winner.

The strange thing is that there was a real sense of destiny about that moment. It didn't feel like Dilbert was being given a name, it felt like I was finding out what his name already was. I can't explain the feeling exactly, except that I knew it was important even then. It was a rare moment of complete clarity, when I knew I was in exactly the right place at the right time.

Much later, after Dilbert became syndicated, Mike realized how he had probably come up with the name. Mike's father had been a navy aviator during World War II and Mike still had some of his old navy documents and publications. In them were some cartoons that were well known to navy pilots of that period—cartoons about an incompetent pilot named Dilbert. The navy Dilbert, by a cartoonist named Osborn, appeared in single panel cartoons used to demonstrate what a pilot should never do by showing what happened when Dilbert did them all.

Had I known about the navy Dilbert cartoons I would have changed the name of mine, but it was too late by that point, happily. I'm glad to carry on the Dilbert tradition, albeit accidentally.

...at Home with Dogbert

HOO-HOO-HEE-HA!

...NO, THAT'S NOT IT.

DO YOU SUPPOSE OTHER PEOPLE PRACTICE LAUGHING WHEN THEY'RE ALONE?

OF COURSE.

TIME FOR YOUR SNEEZING DRILL.

OTHER PEOPLE MAKE IT LOOK SO NATURAL.

At first, Dogbert was the voice of Dilbert's insecurities.

WELL? WHAT DO YOU THINK OF MY NEW POEM?

I ONCE READ THAT GIVEN INFINITE TIME, A THOUSAND MONKEYS WITH TYPEWRITERS WOULD EVENTUALLY WRITE THE ENTIRE WORKS OF SHAKESPEARE.

BUT WHAT ABOUT MY POEM?

THREE MONKEYS, TEN MINUTES.

DO YOU LIKE MY NEW CLIP-ON NECKTIE?

IT'S VERY NICE. GOOD COLORS. NICE PATTERN. WHY, WITH A TIE LIKE THAT, DON'T BE SURPRISED IF YOU GET AN OFFER TO POSE FOR GQ MAGAZINE!

I THINK YOU CROSSED THAT FINE LINE BETWEEN POLITE LYING AND OUTRIGHT SARCASM.

THE MOMENTUM CARRIED ME.

Dogbert's legs were tiny in the beginning.

DILBERT® By Scott Adams

why are homely people discriminated against? we're the _majority_!

12

I shouldn't give away my secrets...to you weasels.

This joke was inspired by a friend who said his house "overlooked a mountain." It's the same pattern. How can you overlook a mountain? They're huge.

I have morning amnesia. I go through this whole routine every day.

13

So many people asked why Dilbert's tie points up that I decided to answer the mystery...

Then I realized I don't know why the tie points up myself. I left it a mystery.

I invented the word "Nerdvana" based on my own computer bliss.

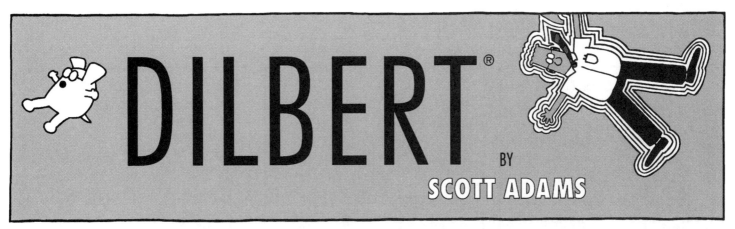

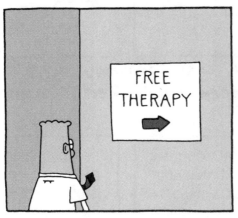

This was part of my early obsession with people who are bad at their jobs.

I'VE HAD NOTHING BUT TRAGEDY SINCE MAKING A FORTUNE IN THE STOCK MARKET.

SOMETIMES, DOGBERT, IT SEEMS LIKE OUR LIVES HAVE PRESET BALANCES OF JOY AND PAIN; WHEN ONE GETS TOO HIGH THE OTHER KICKS IN TO COMPENSATE.

BUT THROUGH IT ALL, I ALWAYS HAVE YOU, MY FRIEND.

AT LEAST UNTIL MY GOOD LUCK KICKS IN.

Dogbert allows me to have the conversations that happen in my head also happen in Dilbert's house.

THE MIGHTY WARRIOR PREPARES FOR BATTLE...

TODAY, BOLD MEMOS WILL BE WRITTEN, DANGEROUS MEETINGS WILL BE ATTENDED, AND MANY A PHOTOCOPIED IMAGE WILL BE CAPTURED FOR ETERNITY.

IF IT WEREN'T FOR SARCASM, MY LIFE WOULD SOUND PATHETIC.

GLAD TO HELP.

I had a boss who always talked in dangerous, war metaphors. It seemed so out of place.

I HAVE AN ETHICAL QUESTION ABOUT TELECOMMUTING, DOGBERT.

DO I OWE MY EMPLOYER EIGHT PRODUCTIVE HOURS, OR DO I ONLY NEED TO MATCH THE TWO PRODUCTIVE HOURS I WOULD HAVE IN THE OFFICE?

WELL, WHEN YOU FACTOR IN HOW YOU'RE SAVING THE PLANET BY NOT DRIVING, YOU ONLY OWE ONE HOUR.

AND THIS MEETING COUNTS.

16

Dogbert is the perfect character to answer any ethical question.

why do beards stop at the neck?
I spend a lot of time wondering that.

ON MY FOURTH DAY OF TELECOMMUTING I REALIZE THAT CLOTHES ARE TOTALLY UNNECESSARY.

SUDDENLY I AM STRUCK BY A QUESTION: WHY DON'T MONKEYS GROW BEARDS?

HEY!

2/9
© 1995 United Feature Syndicate, Inc. (NYC)

I CALL A MEETING TO DISCUSS THE ISSUE BUT ATTENDANCE IS LOW.

ISSUE ONE: MONKEY BEARDS.

LET'S GO AROUND THE TABLE AND INTRODUCE OURSELVES.

. . . and Technology

MY NEW INVENTION SCREENS OUT ALL UNPLEASANT SIGHTS. TRY IT.

WELL, WHAT DO YOU THINK?

S. Adams

WHO SAID THAT?

THE HAND THAT USED TO FEED YOU.

4-21
© 1989 United Feature Syndicate, Inc.

Every invention has a non-obvious down side.

I THINK YOU SHOULD SEE A LAWYER BEFORE UNLEASHING THIS NEW INVENTION ON MANKIND.

LATER...

...I'M AFRAID MY NEW INVENTION WILL EXPOSE ME TO LOTS OF LAWSUITS.

© 1989 United Feature Syndicate, Inc.

S. Adams 5-5

WILL YOU ADVISE ME?

NO. SOUNDS LIKE I CAN MAKE MORE MONEY BY SUING YOU.

17

↰ Loosely based on my lawyer, who hasn't sued me yet.

Broccoli is a funny word. Watch this: "Hey, there's a weasel eating my broccoli!" HA HA HA! ... I kill me.

I was working in a high-tech research department when I wrote this. We would have been lucky to have that parsley invention.

This is an old joke that I cleverly modernized by adding the word "stealth!"

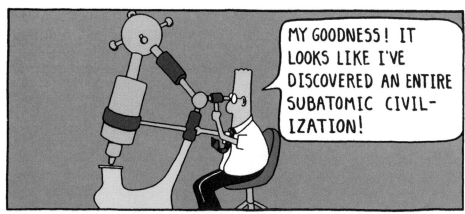

MY GOODNESS! IT LOOKS LIKE I'VE DISCOVERED AN ENTIRE SUBATOMIC CIVILIZATION!

HEY! WHAT ARE YOU STARING AT?!!

I AM DILBERT. I MEAN YOU NO HARM.

For some reason, I find this line very funny. I don't know why.

YOU'RE LOOKING AT THE INCREDIBLY TINY PLANET OF "MINIMUS 6."

MINIMUS 6? THAT MEANS THERE ARE FIVE OTHER PLANETS LIKE YOURS!

S.Adams 7-30

© 1989 United Feature Syndicate, Inc.

LET ME GET YOU FOCUSED A BIT BETTER...

CRUNCH

AND I LOVED THE PART WHEN YOU SAID "I MEAN YOU NO HARM."

I'm often asked what happens when I can't think of anything funny. The fin joke is a good example. What the hell was I thinking?

I had many performance reviews where it was not obvious what value I had created that year.

I prefer jokes where the visuals are in your head, so I don't have to draw anything complicated. How do you draw a denture attack?

WE'RE INVESTIGATING THE DEATH OF YOUR LAB PARTNER.

IT WAS THE FINAL TEST OF THE AUTOMATIC DENTURES... WILLY WASN'T WEARING HIS PROTECTIVE CORN-ON-THE-COB JACKET...

DID YOU NOTICE ANYTHING UNUSUAL?

NO, NOT REALLY.

I think I have killed off more characters than any other cartoonist.

HELLO, ABC NEWS? I'VE DISCOVERED AN ANTI-GRAVITY FORMULA.

WHAT?! IT'S NOT NEWSWORTHY?!

TELL HIM IT LETS YOU LOSE WEIGHT WITHOUT EXERCISING.

ISN'T THAT MISLEADING AND UNETHICAL?

THERE'S A FINE LINE BETWEEN MARKETING AND GRAND THEFT.

Have you ever wondered what makes something "news"?

I SOLD MY ANTI-GRAVITY PATENT TO A COMPANY WHO WANTS TO BRING THE BENEFITS TO THE WORLD.

TIRED OF SAGGING SKIN?

BEFORE AFTER

GET THE PATENTED "DILBERT ANTI-GRAVITY BEAUTY FORMULA!"

YOU MUST BE SO PROUD.

I was sure my editor would put the boot on this cartoon, **21** but she didn't.

I thought the android would become a regular,
but he wasn't as interesting as I'd hoped.

Have you ever squinted to see if maybe you have
X-ray vision. Admit it!

This is why I'm not
a political cartoonist.

MY HOVER-SAUCER INVENTION IS COMPLETE!

IT HAS ENOUGH ADVANCED WEAPONRY TO DESTROY A SMALL COUNTRY.

I HOPE IT DOESN'T FALL INTO THE WRONG HANDS.

PAWS

screwdrivers are the only tools I can draw.

THE GOOD NEWS IS THAT MY HAIR GROWTH FORMULA WORKS.

IN RETROSPECT, I SHOULD HAVE TESTED IT ON MY SCALP INSTEAD OF RUBBING IT ALL OVER MY BODY.

HINDSIGHT...

YEAH...

Do I seem obsessed with hair?

DOGBERT, LOOK, I GOT THE FIRST VIDEO PHONE IN THE CITY!

NOW WE WAIT FOR SOMEBODY ELSE TO BUY A COMPATIBLE VIDEO PHONE AND CALL US.

THE AMAZING THING IS THAT SOCIETY COULDN'T ADVANCE WITHOUT PEOPLE LIKE YOU.

I THINK I SAW SOMETHING.

I actually have an Intel video phone now. I'm waiting for someone **23** *to call.*

WALLY, I NOTICE THAT ALL YOU HAVE IS A PAGER AND A CALCULATOR WATCH.

UH-OH

THAT'S PATHETIC COMPARED TO MY VAST ARRAY OF PERSONAL ELECTRONICS. DO YOU YIELD TO MY TECHNICAL SUPERIORITY?

WHEN A MALE ENGINEER CHALLENGES ANOTHER FOR DOMINANCE OF THE PACK, THERE IS A BRIEF RITUAL-ISTIC BATTLE RARELY SEEN BY OUTSIDERS.

STAY BACK, I'VE GOT A COMPASS!!

WIRELESS FAX!

AAGH!

I had a calculator watch once. I replaced it with a watch that has a TV remote control built in (really)

MY VAST ARRAY OF PERSONAL TECHNOLOGY MAKES ME DOMINANT OVER THE LESS-EQUIPPED ENGINEERS.

I AM SUPERIOR TO THEM ALL... WITH THE POSSIBLE EXCEPTION OF...

TECHNO-BILL !!

LOOKS LIKE SOMEBODY JUST HAD A FAX.

Techno-Bill is the most popular bit player I've ever introduced.

I'VE COMPLETED THE DESIGN FOR BIOWORLD. HAVE YOU SELECTED THE VOLUNTEERS?

YES.

BIOWORLD

SO... THESE ARE THE BRAVE PEOPLE WHOSE LIVES WILL DEPEND ON MY ABILITY TO ENGINEER A BALANCED ECOLOGY.

SEVEN CAR SALESMEN PLUS RATBERT...

COINCIDENCE.

I'm an open-minded guy, but I do hate car salesmen. Does it show?

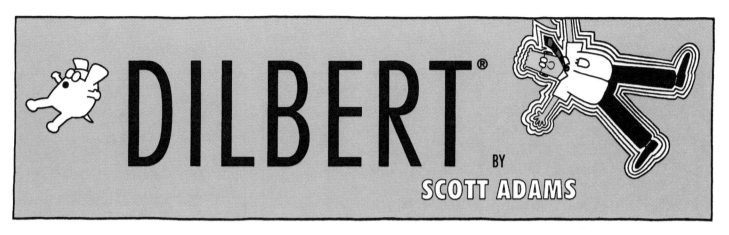

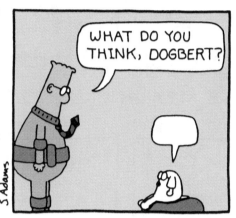

I think I know some people who own these suits already.

HEY, DOGBERT! I JUST DISCOVERED I CAN FIT AN ENTIRE CHANGE OF CLOTHES INTO AN EMPTY "PRINGLES" POTATO CHIP CAN.

12-15

MOST OF THE FABRICS I WEAR CAN BE ROLLED UP PRETTY TIGHT... SO... UH...

IT'S FUNNY HOW THE MOST BRILLIANT IDEA CAN SOUND SILLY WHEN YOU TELL YOUR DOG.

© 1993 United Feature Syndicate, Inc.

This happens to me — I have a great idea and then I make the mistake of telling someone else.

I NEED A NAME FOR MY NEW TUBULAR LUGGAGE INVENTION.

THE NAME SHOULD BE DESCRIPTIVE OF ITS FUNCTION, YET ALSO CALL OUT TO MY TARGET MARKET.

12-16

© 1993 United Feature Syndicate, Inc.

GO AHEAD... GET IT OUT OF YOUR SYSTEM.

"DORKAGE"

You might laugh at this invention, but I'm told that service people roll their clothes to prevent wrinkles when they pack. It could work! Try it at home.

WHAT HAPPENED TO YOUR CLOTHES?

I HAD THEM ROLLED UP AND STUFFED IN A "PRINGLES" POTATO CHIP CAN FOR A WEEK.

© 1993 United Feature Syndicate, Inc.

IT'S A PROTOTYPE FOR MY TUBULAR LUGGAGE INVENTION.

NEVER SPEAK TO ME AGAIN.

12-17

A good name for a band would be "Tubular Luggage."

. . . in the Business World

OH NO... IF THIS GUY TURNS LEFT WHEN I GO RIGHT, WE'LL END UP WALKING DOWN THE HALL RIGHT NEXT TO EACH OTHER.

I HATE THIS... A HUGE, EMPTY HALLWAY AND HERE WE ARE SYNCHRONIZED LIKE TWO OF THE ROCKETTES.

...SO THAT'S WHEN I KNOCKED ON THE LADIES' ROOM DOOR, YELLED "JANITOR" AND DUCKED INSIDE.

AT LEAST YOU MAINTAINED YOUR DIGNITY.

I never know what to do in hallways. There's no graceful solution for shy people like me.

IT'S SO AWKWARD TO WALK PAST STRANGERS IN HALLWAYS; YOU ALWAYS GOTTA AVOID EYE CONTACT.

I KNOW—I'LL WAIT UNTIL WE'RE NEAR AND THEN PICK UP THAT LITTLE PIECE OF FUZZ ON THE CARPET THERE.

...THEN WE BOTH WENT FOR THE CARPET FUZZ.

SMOOTH.

I saw someone do the carpet fuzz trick.

THAT'S RIGHT... COUGH-COUGH! ... I WON'T BE IN TO WORK... COUGH-WHEEZE-COUGH ...

BAD COLD? WELL, NO, ACTUALLY I HAVE A BAD HEADACHE ...

BUT I DON'T KNOW HOW TO MAKE A HEADACHE SOUND OVER THE PHONE.

The best sickness excuse is, "You don't want to know the details."

27

My nose always itches when I speak in public.

HEAR ABOUT THE NEW GUY? HE'S FROM NEW YORK.

GULP✱

HERE HE COMES!

AAGH!

AAAEEEE!!

WELL, I SUPPOSE I COULD HUNT THEM DOWN AND KILL THEM ONE BY ONE.

© 1990 United Feature Syndicate, Inc.

S. Adams

5-5

In California, we fear people from New York City.

DILBERT, I'M PUTTING YOU IN CHARGE OF THE DEPARTMENT SECRETARY.

S. Adams

7-10

© 1990 United Feature Syndicate, Inc.

SEE IF YOU CAN GET HIM TO CUT DOWN ON THE PERSONAL PHONE CALLS.

... JUST BE A LITTLE MORE DISCREET... FOR EXAMPLE, TRY NOT WEARING THE TRADITIONAL COSTUME OF THE COUNTRIES YOU'RE CALLING.

I worked with this secretary.

I JOINED THE "SCIENTIST ANTI-DEFAMATION LEAGUE."

WHAT'S THAT?

S. Adams

THEY FIGHT AGAINST THE NEGATIVE STEREOTYPES OF TECHNICAL PEOPLE THAT ARE OFTEN PORTRAYED IN THE MEDIA.

© 1991 United Feature Syndicate, Inc.

YOU BROKE MY CONCENTRATION.

1-21

I did this cartoon after getting a complaint letter from a scientist.

29

WELCOME TO THE "SCIENTIST ANTI-DEFAMATION LEAGUE" WEEKLY MEETING.

TONIGHT'S TOPIC IS THE STEREOTYPE THAT WE SCIENTISTS HAVE NO SOCIAL LIVES...

BUT FIRST...

IS SATURDAY NIGHT OKAY FOR OUR NEXT MEETING?

I'M FREE

NO PROBLEM

WIDE OPEN

I'm not smart enough to be a scientist, so I make my living by mocking them.

STARTING TODAY, THE COMPANY WILL BEGIN RANDOM DRUG TESTING.

ALTHOUGH IT WOULD BE ILLEGAL TO SEARCH YOUR CAR OR HOME FOR ILLEGAL DRUGS...

WE HAVE FOUND NO ETHICAL PROBLEM WITH SUCKING THE BLOOD OUT OF YOUR BODY.

RESULTS WILL BE POSTED IN THE CAFETERIA.

I'm amazed that this is legal in the USA.

IT'S AN ETHICAL DILEMMA... I SUPPORT MY COMPANY'S GOAL OF DISCOURAGING DRUG USE, BUT THE RANDOM DRUG TESTING POLICY IS A VIOLATION OF MY CONSTITUTIONAL RIGHTS.

I'LL GET FIRED IF I REFUSE THE TEST. WHAT IS THE ETHICAL THING TO DO?

HACK INTO THEIR COMPUTER AND CHANGE YOUR BOSS'S TEST RESULTS.

SOMETIMES THE STRAIGHTEST PATH IS THROUGH THE MUD.

GOOD, RATIONALIZE IT WITH AN OBTUSE METAPHOR.

A good metaphor can make any bad idea sound good.

DILBERT®

By Scott Adams

THIS CONCLUDES MY PROPOSAL TO THE EXECUTIVE COMMITTEE. ANY QUESTIONS?

NO, I THINK MOST OF US WERE THINKING ABOUT OTHER THINGS.

BUT HERE'S MY IMPRESSION OF WHAT YOU LOOKED LIKE GIVING THE PRESENTATION.

© 1991 United Feature Syndicate, Inc.

FUH FUH FUH FUH

NO, NO, IT WAS MORE LIKE...

FUH FUH FUH FUH

HOW DID YOUR PRESENTATION GO?

DON'T ASK.

FUH FUH DON'T ASK FUH FUH FUH FUH...

S. Adams

4-21

This cartoon is based on the most evil executive I ever met. He actually mocked people this way.

31

I should have put "velcro" in quotes because it's a trademark. Oops.

When I ate lunch with the engineers at Pacific Bell, the one-upping continued until the food was all gone.

The more I exaggerate a character, the more he's familiar. It's strange.

HI, LES.

YOU SAY THAT ALMOST MOCKINGLY.

THE WAY YOU SAY IT, MY NAME SOUNDS LIKE "LESS." I'VE TOLD YOU A MILLION TIMES IT'S FRENCH -- PRONOUNCED "LEZ."

YOU SEEM A LITTLE SHORT-TEMPERED.

HEY! THAT TIME YOU DID IT ON PURPOSE!!

Yes, I did get complaints from the vertically challenged.

DILBERT, THIS IS YOUR NEW CO-WORKER, FLOYD REMORA.

FLOYD HAS WORKED HERE FOR TWENTY YEARS WITH-OUT DEVELOPING ANY SKILLS. HE SURVIVES BY ATTACHING HIMSELF TO THE BACKS OF OTHER EMPLOYEES.

GO AHEAD... ASK ME HOW MY DAY WENT.

This is perhaps the weirdest character I've ever created. He's based on a particular co-worker I once had.

I HOPE YOU WON'T MIND MY PILLOW AND BLANKET AT YOUR PRESENTA-TION.

THE LAST TIME YOU PRESENTED, I LOST CONSCIOUSNESS AND BROKE MY NOSE ON THE TABLE.

WHATEVER HAPPENED TO GOOD MANNERS?

ZZZ ZZZ
Bonk
Bonk
ZZZ Bonk
ZZZ

I've known people who could sleep during meetings with no sense of shame. I envy them.

33

HEY, MISTER, WAKE UP!

HUH?

IT WAS ALL A DREAM! YOU'RE NOT A DUMPY ENGINEER -- YOU'RE REALLY A PLAYBOY MILLIONAIRE MOVIE STAR!!

I...I AM??

I LOVE BEING THE NIGHT JANITOR.

THEN WHY DO I DRESS LIKE THIS?

© 1991 United Feature Syndicate, Inc.

Sleeping at work is a common theme in Dilbert. I used to sleep in my cubicle all the time.

UH-OH, NARDO IS COMING. I'M OUT OF HERE.

UH, HI, NARDO.

IN THE OLD COUNTRY WE DID NOT HAVE WHAT YOU CALL PERSONAL SPACE.

TAKE YOUR HANDS OUT OF MY POCKETS.

OH, I GET IT. THEY'RE FOR YOUR USE ONLY, RIGHT?

© 1991 United Feature Syndicate, Inc.

I was raised in the country, where touching means you're standing on the same carpet. Any closer and you're engaged.

FROM NOW ON, ALL EMPLOYEES ARE EMPOWERED TO MAKE THEIR OWN DECISIONS.

EMPOWERMENT IS THE CONCEPT OF THE NINETIES. YOU'LL BE HAPPIER AND MORE PRODUCTIVE.

YOU'RE FIRED, DILBERT.

NO, YOU ARE!

I'LL NEVER WORK HARD AGAIN!

© 1991 United Feature Syndicate, Inc.

Empowerment might be the all-time dumbest idea, at least when it's over-applied.

DILBERT, I'M PUTTING YOU ON A ROTATIONAL ASSIGNMENT...

YOU WILL BE WORKING IN MARKETING UNTIL FURTHER NOTICE.

MARKETING
TWO DRINK MINIMUM

When I worked in Engineering, the marketing department was our evil nemesis.

DILBERT IS TRANSFERRED TO MARKETING

YOU LOOK LOST.

I NEVER KNEW THAT MARKETING WAS LIKE THIS... DO YOU PEOPLE DO ANY WORK?

WELL, NOT ON "BARBECUE TUESDAY." ARE YOU STAYING FOR LUNCH? IT'S UNICORN!

It always seemed like Marketing had all of the party people.

DILBERT IS TRANSFERRED TO MARKETING

EVERY TUESDAY WE BARBECUE A UNICORN.

MAKE MINE RARE. HA HA! GET IT? RARE?

I'M NOT SURE I BELIEVE THIS IS THE "BEST PART."

I got complaints from unicorn lovers.

This joke was written by a reader as part of a fill-in-the-punchline contest. So don't blame me.

Some of my Pacific Bell co-workers longed for jobs where they would never be noticed.

I'm 5'8" and it bugs me when big oafs don't look where they're going.

...SO THEN I SPENT A YEAR IN EUROPE AND BLAH BLAH BLAH BLAH.

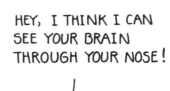

HEY, I THINK I CAN SEE YOUR BRAIN THROUGH YOUR NOSE!

ANYWAY... YOU WERE SAYING..?

I always say the wrong thing, usually because I'm bored.

IT LOOKS LIKE BRENDA HAS BEEN BRAINWASHED BY THE NEW COMPANY SLOGAN.

QUALITY... QUALITY...

IT ALL STARTED WHEN WE GOT THESE LITTLE STICKY NOTE PADS THAT SAY "QUALITY" ON THEM.

OOPS, SORRY, I SHOULDN'T PUT IT RIGHT IN YOUR FACE...

QUALITY... QUALITY... QUALITY...

I was part of a "Quality" initiative where the only tangible change was to our notepads.

GEE, TIM, YOU LOOK AWFUL.

I'VE BEEN WORKING FOR FIVE DAYS WITHOUT ANY SLEEP TO FINISH THIS REPORT.

AT FIRST I HAD A MENTAL BLOCK. BUT ON THE FOURTH DAY I WAS VISITED BY AN INCAN MONKEY GOD WHO TOLD ME WHAT TO WRITE.

WOW, LUCKY BREAK.

NOW I JUST HAVE TO FIND SOMEBODY WHO CAN TRANSLATE HIS SIMPLE BUT BEAUTIFUL LANGUAGE.

I had a co-worker who didn't realize how much the quality of her **37** output was influenced by sleep deprivation.

I have to say "Camp Girl" instead of using a real organization's name. We fear them.

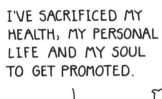

I'VE SACRIFICED MY HEALTH, MY PERSONAL LIFE AND MY SOUL TO GET PROMOTED.

HA HA HA! BUT IT WAS ALL WORTH IT BECAUSE I HAVE AN OFFICE WITH A <u>DOOR</u> AND YOU STILL WORK IN A CUBICLE!

MAYBE I'LL HOST A SPECIAL "LOW-ACHIEVER DAY" TO LET YOU TOUCH MY DOOR.

OOPS

I spent most of my career in corporate America suffering from door envy.

HEY, I HAVEN'T DONE A THING FOR MINUTES AND YET I STILL GET PAID.

HOO-HOO-HA! I'M RIPPING OFF THE EVIL CORPORATE EMPIRE AND THERE'S NOTHING THEY CAN DO ABOUT IT! I HAVE TOTAL POWER!

I'D BETTER KEEP THIS LITTLE SECRET TO MYSELF.

HEY, I'M GETTING PAID FOR DOING NOTHING!

I relished the small revenges.

AT THE "RIVERS AND TREES" MANAGEMENT COURSE.

WE'LL START WITH A TRUST-BUILDING EXERCISE.

YOU HAVE ONE MINUTE TO DECIDE TO EAT THESE DONUTS OR TO SAVE YOUR CO-WORKER FROM THE BEAR.

OKAY, WHO WANTS TO BE ON THE DONUT OPTION WORKING COMMITTEE?

OOPS... PROBLEM SOLVED.

This was inspired by my own tragic experiences at "team building."

AT THE "RIVERS AND TREES" MANAGEMENT COURSE.

THIS NEXT EXERCISE IS ALWAYS A FAVORITE.

USING ONLY A ROPE, YOUR TEAM MUST FIGURE OUT HOW TO CROSS THE MUDDY PATCH WITHOUT GETTING YOUR FEET DIRTY.

I COULD HAVE BEEN A FOREST RANGER, BUT NO-O-O-O...

It's hard to draw mud!

WHAT HAPPENED TO YOU?

I ASKED FLOYD A QUESTION.

FLOYD HATES HIS JOB, SO HE TAKES IT OUT ON CO-WORKERS. HE ALMOST CHEWED MY CLOTHES OFF.

HOW'D YOU STOP HIM?

HE WENT INTO SYNTHETIC SHOCK; IT'S NOT HEALTHY TO EAT TOO MUCH OF THIS STUFF.

I favor the death penalty for any co-worker who intentionally causes discomfort.

WHAT?! YOU THINK I'LL HELP YOU JUST BECAUSE I'M YOUR CO-WORKER?? HA! I HATE CO-WORKERS!

ALL I NEED IS...

I HATE THIS JOB! I HATE EVERYTHING! THE ONLY THING I LIKE IS BEING MEAN TO CO-WORKERS WHO NEED THE VITAL INFORMATION THAT I CONTROL!

IF YOU THINK YOU HATE HIM, YOU SHOULD TRY BEING HIS SECRETARY.

In every job, there was always one of these guys.

40

EVERYBODY PICK A STRAW. THE LOSER HAS TO KILL OUR ABUSIVE CO-WORK-ER, FLOYD.

DILBERT LOSES. HE PICKED THE BLUE STRAW.

I THOUGHT THE SHORT STRAW LOSES.

YOU'RE ALREADY A MURDERER; DON'T BE A CHEAT-ER TOO.

It's a common fantasy to bump off an obnoxious co-worker. (or is it just me?)

SO... DILBERT, WELCOME TO THE SALES DEPART-MENT. I'M TINA, YOUR NEW BOSS.

HI

AS THE NEW GUY, YOU GET THE CUSTOMERS WHO DESPISE OUR PRODUCTS AND WANT TO HURT US PERSONALLY.

I HATE YOU! I HATE YOU!

YOU'LL BE SELL-ING TO THE SMALL BUSINESS MARKET. HE'S YOUR BEST ACCOUNT.

This is why I don't work in sales.

DILBERT THE SALESMAN...

YOUR COMPETITOR WAS HERE AN HOUR AGO...

HE PROMISED ME A MASSAGE FROM HELGA IF I BUY FROM HIS COMPANY. WHAT'S YOUR OFFER?

I'LL GIVE YOU MY HOUSE FOR HELGA.

YOU'RE NEW AT THIS...

I used to quiz engineers about why they carry so many writing tools at once. As far as I can tell, it's so they'll have emergency backups.

DILBERT HAS AGREED TO TALK TO THE CLASS ABOUT EXCITING CAREERS IN THE FIELD OF ENGINEERING!

THERE'S MORE TO BEING AN ENGINEER THAN JUST WRITING TECHNICAL MEMOS THAT NOBODY READS.

4-20

ONCE IN A WHILE, SOME-BODY READS ONE. THEN YOU HAVE TO FIND A SCAPEGOAT, OR USE SOME VACATION TIME AND HOPE IT ALL BLOWS OVER.

I never knew what an engineer did for a living when I was a kid. I still don't.

DILBERT TALKS TO A CLASS ABOUT CAREER OPTIONS.

ENGINEERING IS ONE OF THE BEST CAREERS AVAILABLE.

FOR THE NEXT TWENTY YEARS I'LL SIT IN A BIG BOX CALLED A CUBICLE. IT'S LIKE A RESTROOM STALL BUT WITH LOWER WALLS.

4-21

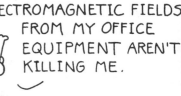

I SPEND MOST OF MY TIME HOPING THE ELECTROMAGNETIC FIELDS FROM MY OFFICE EQUIPMENT AREN'T KILLING ME.

It's a good thing that nobody tells kids what work is really like.

DILBERT TALKS TO A CLASS ABOUT CAREER OPTIONS.

THE GOAL OF EVERY ENGINEER IS TO RETIRE WITHOUT GETTING BLAMED FOR A MAJOR CATASTROPHE.

ENGINEERS PREFER TO WORK AS "CONSULTANTS" ON PROJECT TEAMS. THAT WAY THERE'S NO REAL WORK, BLAME IS SPREAD ACROSS THE GROUP, AND YOU CAN CRUSH ANY IDEA FROM MARKETING!

4-23

...AND SOMETIMES YOU GET FREE DONUTS JUST FOR SHOWING UP!

GET OUT OF MY CLASS-ROOM.

 This is more truth than exaggeration.

43

The guy in the cubicle across the hall from me coined the phrase "sensory deprivation chamber" for his cubicle. I liked it.

You say bologna, I say baloney.

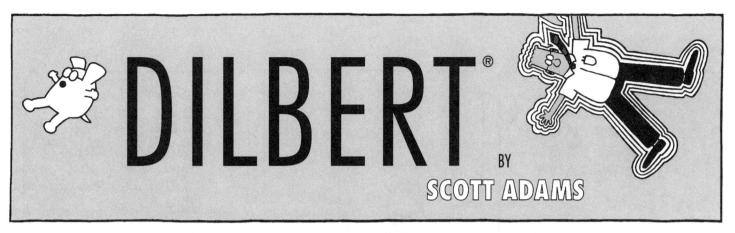

DILBERT
BY SCOTT ADAMS

THE AWARD FOR BEST ATTENDANCE GOES TO DILBERT.

I'D LIKE TO THANK THE PEOPLE WHO MADE THIS POSSIBLE.

FIRST, I'D LIKE TO THANK THE WOMEN IN THE COMPANY WHO HAVE REJECTED ME OVER THE YEARS...

BECAUSE OF THEM I HAVE NO GERM-RIDDLED CHILDREN TO INFECT ME.

AND THANKS TO MY CO-WORKERS FOR NEVER TELLING ME ABOUT IMPORTANT MEETINGS, THUS KEEPING MY GERM EXPOSURE TO A MINIMUM.

AND THANKS TO MY BOSS FOR NEVER ASSIGNING A PROJECT IMPORTANT ENOUGH TO INDUCE STRESS AND WEAKEN MY IMMUNE SYSTEM.

BUT WHAT MAKES THIS AWARD SPECIAL IS THAT EACH OF YOU HAD TO GET SICK IN ORDER FOR ME TO WIN.

WHEN YOU HAVE YOUR HEALTH, YOU HAVE EVERYTHING, DOGBERT.

NO, YOU ALSO HAVE TO GLOAT.

© 1993 United Feature Syndicate, Inc.

7-18

45

I like the phrase "germ-riddled children."

Yes, I __know__ there's no such thing as the Vulcan death grip, even on "Star Trek."

Every company is better than your own. It's a rule of the universe.

↖ Note the elaborate use of background.

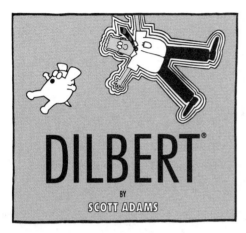

DILBERT
BY SCOTT ADAMS

YOU ALL KNOW OUR PRESIDENT, MISTER GOODENRICH. HE'S HERE TO ANSWER ANY QUESTIONS YOU HAVE.

WHY AREN'T THERE ANY WOMEN OR MINORITIES IN SENIOR MANAGEMENT POSITIONS?

WE THINK WOMEN ARE FOR MAKING BABIES. AS FOR MINORITIES, WE FEAR THEM.

HOW CAN YOU JUSTIFY YOUR TEN MILLION DOLLAR SALARY WHEN PROFITS ARE DOWN?

HA HA! THE BOARD OF DIRECTORS ARE FRIENDS OF MINE AND IT'S NOT THEIR MONEY THEY'RE SPENDING.

WHY DOES THE COMPANY KEEP TALKING ABOUT EMPLOYEE TRAINING WHILE AT THE SAME TIME SLASHING THE TRAINING BUDGET?

WE THINK YOU'RE TOO DUMB TO TRAIN. WE'LL HIRE PEOPLE FROM THE OUTSIDE IF WE NEED TALENT.

I MUST SAY, YOUR HONESTY IS KIND OF REFRESHING.

AND YOU'RE ALL FIRED FOR ASKING QUESTIONS.

There's a reason that executives lie. The alternative is worse!

DILBERT THE MENTOR

THIS IS YOUR COMPUTER.

WHEN YOU HEAR FOOTSTEPS IT'S A GOOD IDEA TO MOVE THIS THING AROUND AND CLICK IT.

THIS CONCLUDES YOUR TECHNICAL TRAINING. IF YOU HAVE FURTHER QUESTIONS JUST REMEMBER YOU'RE INCONVENIENCING ME.

when people are mentored, they do in fact hold their arms out like that.

BOOM!

CRASH!

I HEAR YOUR COMPANY IS TRIMMING TRAVEL BUDGETS.

CAN ANY-ONE LEND ME BUS FARE TO GET HOME?

This is a rare action-oriented strip. I don't do many because they take longer.

I...I'D LIKE PERMISSION TO KEEP A PLASTIC PLANT IN MY CUBICLE.

CUBICLE GESTAPO

PERMISSION DENIED! PLANTS ATTRACT BUGS. IF I CAN'T TELL IT'S PLASTIC HOW ARE THE BUGS GOING TO KNOW THE DIFFERENCE?

WITH ALL DUE RESPECT, BUGS ARE WAY SMARTER THAN YOU.

OH YEAH? I'D LIKE TO SEE THEM DO THIS JOB.

when this appeared in papers, we changed "Gestapo" **48** to "police" to avoid complaints.

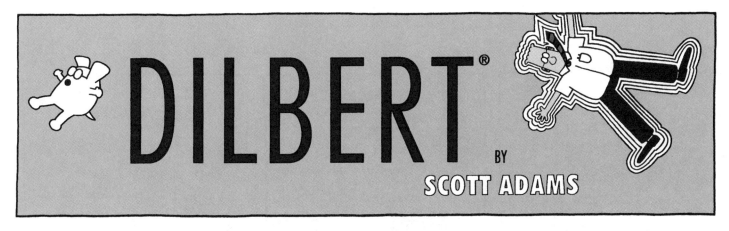

DILBERT®

BY **SCOTT ADAMS**

My publisher adds the color to these. They pick the worst possible times to add diversity to the cast.

HAVE A NICE NIGHT, DILBERT.

YOU CAN REST EASY KNOWING I'LL BE GUARDING THE BUILDING ALL NIGHT.

TO A CRIMINAL, THIS PLACE MUST LOOK LIKE A BIG OL' SHOPPING MALL.

THE CUBICLES ARE LIKE LITTLE STORES, EACH WITH ITS OWN SELECTION OF QUALITY MERCHANDISE.

IF YOU KNEW WHERE TO LOOK, YOU COULD GET PICTURE FRAMES, POSTAGE STAMPS, CLOCKS, AND EVEN FOOTWEAR.

ODDLY ENOUGH, YOU AND THE JANITOR ARE THE ONLY ONES HERE AT NIGHT, AND YET MY SNACK DRAWER KEEPS GETTING EMPTIED.

10-24

IT'S TOTALLY INEXPLICABLE.

WELL, GOOD NIGHT.

SHALL WE HEAD OVER TO "CHEZ DILBERT"?

LATER... THERE'S A SALE AT "WALLY'S SHOE WORLD."

We used "police" instead of "Gestapo" for newspapers on this one too.

By this time I was having serious hand problems, so the lettering was being inked by another artist. My hand got much better, but I continued this method to save time.

Casual clothes are a double-edged sword.

I REALIZE THAT CASUAL DRESS DAY ISN'T EASY FOR YOU ENGINEERS...

BUT YOU'VE EXCEEDED THE BOUNDS OF GOOD TASTE. I'VE GOT TO SEND YOU HOME TO CHANGE.

SHUT UP, WALLY.

I HEARD THEY WERE BACK! I SWEAR!

I get more requests for casual day jokes than for any other topic.

ACCORDING TO YOU, IF I CUT YOUR BUDGET THE WORLD WILL ABRUPTLY STOP SPINNING AND WE'LL BE FLUNG INTO SPACE.

WHEREAS, THE RISK OF CUTTING DILBERT'S PROJECT IS "...A PLAGUE OF LOCUSTS O'ER THE LAND."

I'LL CUT BOTH PROJECTS. WITH ANY LUCK, WE'LL FLING THE LOCUSTS INTO SPACE.

LOCUSTS. REAL GOOD.

I was never good at protecting my budget because I was a terrible liar.

SOMETIMES I THINK THESE CONSTANT REORGANIZATIONS ARE JUST EXCUSES FOR GETTING RID OF UNWANTED EMPLOYEES.

WHAT JOB DID YOU END UP WITH?

ORGAN DONOR.

MY SHOULDER IS ACTING UP. DO I TALK TO YOU OR IS THERE A FORM TO FILL OUT?

I DON'T THINK THAT'S AN "ORGAN."

↰ You know it's true!

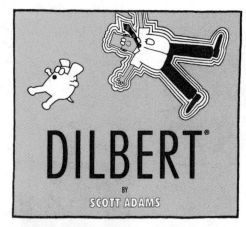

The pager-in-the-toilet problem is real. I've heard lots of stories about it.

Panel 1: OUR DEVICE CONFORMS TO ALL INTERNATIONAL STANDARDS FOR COMMUNICATIONS.

Panel 2: IN OTHER WORDS, IT DOESN'T DO ANYTHING USEFUL AND IT'S NOT YOUR FAULT.

4-11

Panel 3: IS THERE SOMEBODY LESS EXPERIENCED I COULD TALK TO?

DO YOU HAVE MY BOSS'S NUMBER?

I never draw these side view mouths anymore. →    Now I do these →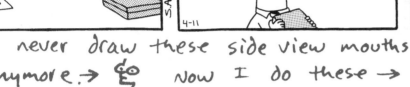

Panel 4: THP·P·P·P

Panel 5: I CAN'T HEAR YOU! LA-LA-LA-LA-HM-HM-LA-LA

Panel 6: HE'S RIGHT! IT IS JUST LIKE A LITTLE FORT!!

FRIDAY MEETINGS.

4-29

I've never accomplished anything during a Friday meeting (except getting comic fodder).

Panel 7: WE COULD HAVE OUR NEXT ALL-DAY STAFF MEETING AT MY HOUSE.

Panel 9: DO YOU HAVE ACTUAL FURNITURE?

SOMEBODY WILL HAVE TO SIT IN THE BATHROOM.

I CALL BATHROOM

5-2

Everywhere I've lived, visitors look at my home **53** and say, "Did you just move in?"

HOW FOOLISH OF YOU TO HOST THE ALL-DAY STAFF MEETING AT YOUR HOUSE.

LET'S FORM SUB-TEAMS TO BE MORE EFFICIENT. TED WILL DO ACCIDENTAL SPILLS. ALICE, YOU CRITIQUE THE DECOR. I'LL BE A FLOATER.

KITCHEN, SHODDILY DONE...

I SPILLED MAYONAISE ON THE WALL.

WHERE'S THE BATH-ROOM?

Wally looks so cute in a jacket.

I'M PUTTING YOU IN CHARGE OF AN IMPORTANT PROJECT WHICH IS FULLY FUNDED.

GASBY?

I'M A MARKED MAN. THE OTHER EMPLOYEES WILL EITHER TRY TO SUCK UP TO ME FOR MONEY OR THROW BRICKS AT ME.

BUDDY!

THE TRICK IS TO KEEP A PROTECTIVE RING OF SUCK-UPS AROUND AT ALL TIMES.

ZIP!

I had a project with a big budget once. It was like "Night of the Living Dead" as the zombies surrounded me.

I AM THE KING OF MY CUBICLE, THE ABSOLUTE RULER OF THIS TINY REALM.

AND THESE ARE MY LOYAL SUBJECTS: MISTER COMPUTER, MISTER STAPLER, AND THE BINDER FAMILY.

WHO SPILLED COFFEE?

THE BARBARIAN IS THWARTED AT THE MOAT.

Dilbert is the kind of guy who makes the best of a situation.

DILBERT®

BY
SCOTT ADAMS

LAURIE'S OUR NEW ENGINEER. SHOW HER THE ROPES, DILBERT.

I MEANT FIGURATIVELY.

THIS IS YOUR ANTI-PRODUCTIVITY POD.

IT'S EQUIPPED WITH A LITTLE DEVICE THAT RINGS ANYTIME YOU TRY TO CONCENTRATE.

THE TOP IS OPEN SO NONE OF THE BACKGROUND NOISE IS INADVERTENTLY MUFFLED.

AND YOU'RE ON THE MAIN AISLE, SO YOU'LL BE HAUNTED EVERY MINUTE BY FOOTSTEPS BEHIND YOU ... STEP... STEP... STEP...

WE NEED TO TALK.

I believe cubicles were invented by someone who didn't like people.

when engineers eat bananas, it destroys their credibility.

As a rule, anything in a binder has very little value, except as building material.

↰ This happened to me often.

This exact thing happened to me, not counting the attractive outfit.

I experimented with doing my lettering by computer. In the end it was easier to have a human do it. Readers complained about the regularity of this lettering.

The urge goes away in the fifth year, typically. Never work in the same place for five years.

Every group has a pathological liar.

WE'RE ANNOUNCING TWO NEW PROGRAMS FOR EMPLOYEES.

THE FIRST IS A NEW DIGNITY ENHANCEMENT PROGRAM AND THE SECOND IS OUR NEW RANDOM DRUG TESTING INITIATIVE.

THE CLUE METER IS READING ZERO.

YOU EACH GET A HANDSOME COFFEE MUG AS PART OF THE KICK-OFF.

Motorola employees suggested this plot, which is loosely based on their company.

DROP YOUR TROUSERS AND TURN AROUND. I NEED A DNA SAMPLE.

WE'RE SCANNING FOR ANY FATAL GENETIC PROBLEMS THAT COULD HURT PRODUCTIVITY.

UH... WE DECIDED TO MOVE YOUR PROJECT DEADLINE UP A WEEK.

This day will come.

WE NEED TO FINISH YOUR PROGRAM TWICE AS FAST, SO I'M ADDING A PERSON TO HELP YOU.

YOU MIGHT NEED TO TRAIN HIM A LITTLE BEFORE HE'S PRODUCTIVE.

WARNING! WARNING! DR. SMITH

TELL ME AGAIN WHAT THE BIG GLOWING THING IS.

should have been ↑ "Mr." Smith, a
reference to the
old "Lost in Space" TV show.

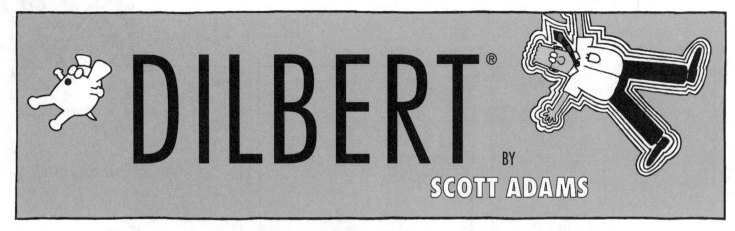

Garbage bags are often used
this way in the seattle area. **60**
They call it an "Engineer's Raincoat."

JUST AS I THOUGHT, MY CUBICLE IS TWO INCHES SMALLER TODAY THAN YESTERDAY!

WE INSTALLED REAL-TIME STATUS ADJUSTERS IN THE CUBICLE WALLS. SENSORS MONITOR YOUR WORK AND ADJUST THE CUBICLE SIZE ACCORDING TO YOUR VALUE.

IT'S AMAZING HOW FAST YOU GET USED TO IT.

At Digital Equipment Corporation they call this process "Densification!"

EFFECTIVE IMMEDIATELY, WE WILL NO LONGER USE OUR SPARE CUBICLES TO HOUSE CONVICTS.

YES!!! OUR OPINIONS MATTERED!

ACTUALLY, IT'S BECAUSE THE PRISONERS COMPLAINED.

I WONDER WHAT HE PLANS TO DO WITH THE SPARE CUBICLES NOW.

cubicles are better than maximum-security prisons, but about the same as minimum-security, I'll bet.

TODAY WE HAVE A MOTIVATIONAL SPEAKER FROM THE "DISCOUNT SPEAKERS BUREAU."

YOU SHOULD, LIKE, WORK HARDER... OTHERWISE YOU MIGHT GET FIRED. ANY QUESTIONS?

WOULD WE GET BONUSES FOR WORKING HARDER?

THIS MUST BE THE SLOW CLASS.

I like to put opposites together. I've heard stories about motivational speakers who depress people.

WHO NEEDS TO SIGN MY BUSINESS CASE TO BUY A WEB SERVER?

HMM...THIS CROSSES ALL DEPARTMENTS. I FEAR IT. GET THE APPROVAL OF EVERY DIRECTOR, EVERY VP, EVERY EVP, PLUS GRIFFIN.

DO YOU MEAN TED GRIFFIN IN FINANCE OR THE MYTHICAL GRIFFIN BEAST THAT'S HALF EAGLE, HALF LION?

WHICHEVER IS HARDER.

... and Women

I heard from lots of people named Griffin.

I CAN REMEMBER WHEN THESE WERE ONLY FIFTEEN CENTS.

BUT I'M REALLY DATING MYSELF NOW...

WELL, IT'S NOT AS IF ANYBODY ELSE WOULD DATE YOU.

This is the very first Dilbert strip published. The setup line is something I heard from a lonely engineer. The punchline I kept to myself.

THERE... MY PROGRAM PROVES THAT PRETTY WOMEN HAVE EXTREMELY BAD PERSONALITIES.

THIS IS BASED ON THE INPUT THAT PRETTY WOMEN ARE NEVER NICE TO ME.

WHY DOES THE SCREEN SAY, "OR YOU ARE A GEEK"?

DARN! I THOUGHT I FIXED THAT BUG.

This was based on my personal experience.

I was just starting as a cartoonist and hadn't decided how to draw women's faces at this point.

I'VE DESIGNED THIS PROGRAM TO GENERATE THE MOST EFFECTIVE PICK-UP LINE IN THE UNIVERSE.

HA HA! WOMEN WILL BE HELPLESS WHEN THEY HEAR MY CLEVER OPENER.

...AND THE LINE IS...

"HI. I'M MEL GIBSON. DID YOU SEE A DINGO DOG GO BY HERE WITH MY SHIRT?"

KISS ME, YOU WICKED SAVAGE.

Anything with the words "Dingo dog" is funny.

I'VE GOT A BLIND DATE WITH THE LADY WHO WORKS AT THE LIBRARY REFERENCE DESK.

WHAT IF SHE'S UGLY?

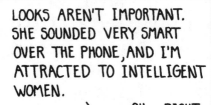

LOOKS AREN'T IMPORTANT. SHE SOUNDED VERY SMART OVER THE PHONE, AND I'M ATTRACTED TO INTELLIGENT WOMEN.

OH...RIGHT.

UH...SHOULD I TALK, OR WILL YOU BE READING MY THOUGHTS DIRECTLY?

I had some blind dates in my dating days.
I would have been happy with this outcome.

I CAN TELL WHAT MY DATE IS THINKING BY HER BODY LANGUAGE.

HER BODY IS TELLING ME "LET'S CUDDLE BY A FIREPLACE..."

"I'LL GET SOME FIREWOOD," SHE SAYS...

VROOOOM

If men were perceptive,
they'd never get lucky.

RIDING ELEVATORS IS SO AWKWARD

STARE STRAIGHT AHEAD... DON'T BREATHE... DON'T FIDGET... DON'T BLINK... ARMS HANG LIKE LIMP WEIGHTS...

I THINK HE'S DEAD.

ABOVE ALL, ACT NATURALLY.

I've actually stopped breathing in elevators because I think it sounds loud.

I WILL NEVER GO ON ANOTHER BLIND DATE.

SO, JABBA ... ER... I MEAN, JANET, HAVE YOU DATED MANY OTHER MEN?

YES, BUT THEY ALL DISAPPEARED WITHOUT A TRACE.

INCIDENTALLY, YOU LOOK DELICIOUS TONIGHT.

I took a lot of heat for this cartoon. I meant it to be about a woman who was gigantic in general, but it comes off as a fat joke.

SO...UH... WHY DID YOU DECIDE TO TAKE UP WITCH-CRAFT?

IT COMES IN HANDY.

FOR EXAMPLE, SUPPOSE I WANT TO GET RID OF THIS ANNOYING FLY HERE.

NOW BE A LUV...

Do frogs have
65 noses? They're
hard to draw.

TO ME, A WOMAN IS LIKE A FINE BOTTLE OF WINE.

EACH ONE IS FAMILIAR, YET DISTINCTIVE AND SPECIAL.

IN THE WINE OF LIFE, SOME PEOPLE ARE DESTINED TO BE CORK-SNIFFERS.

This sounds naughtier than it is.

THIS IS ABSOLUTELY THE LAST BLIND DATE.

...THEN I REALIZED...

I'M A WOMAN TRAPPED IN A DOG'S BODY... SO, NOW I'M SAVING FOR A SPECIES CHANGE OPERATION.

IS IT EXPENSIVE?

WELL, YOU CAN IMAGINE THE ELECTROLYSIS COSTS ALONE...

Talking dogs are funny.

I GUESS A GOOD NIGHT KISS IS OUT OF THE QUESTION.

FETCH!

THAT ENDED MORE GRACE-FULLY THAN MOST OF MY DATES.

what do you do at the end of a bad date?

DILBERT

By Scott Adams

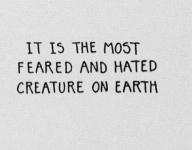

IT IS THE MOST FEARED AND HATED CREATURE ON EARTH

© 1991 United Feature Syndicate, Inc.

NOT A DINOSAUR

GRRRR

NOT A RABID DOG

RABID?

NOT DONALD TRUMP

IT IS THE "UGLY SINGLE MALE"

OTHER MALES FEAR BEING ASSOCIATED WITH HIM

HI, GUYS!

WOMEN AVOID EYE CONTACT AND FLEE IN HORROR

ANYBODY FREE FOR LUNCH?

ONLY A MAIDEN SACRIFICE CAN END THE HORROR

WE DREW STRAWS; I HAVE TO MARRY YOU.

The original text said "virgin" not "maiden."
It was softened so it wouldn't draw
complaints in conservative towns.

I MUST WARN YOU THAT I HAVE AN OBSESSIVE PERSONALITY.

IF I SPEND A MOMENT WITH A MAN I FALL COMPLETELY IN LOVE. I THINK OF ONLY HIM. I... I BECOME HIS SLAVE.

ARE YOU SAYING...

YES. I'M IN LOVE WITH OUR WAITER.

Nice lips, eh?

BELIEVE IT OR NOT, THIS IS THE FIRST TIME I'VE EVER DATED A TWO-HEADED TELEPATH.

YOU MIGHT PICK UP A STRANGE THOUGHT OR TWO, BUT BELIEVE ME, THESE ARE NORMAL THOUGHTS FOR A GUY...

WELL, MAYBE NOT THAT LAST ONE...

It's a good thing women have no idea what men think.

LISA, I WAS WONDERING IF YOU'D LIKE TO GO OUT TO DINNER SATURDAY NIGHT.

UH... I HAVE TO WASH MY HAIR SATURDAY. HOW ABOUT HAVING COFFEE HERE AT WORK INSTEAD?

I'LL PASS. I WAS HOPING FOR SOMEONE WITH CLEAN HAIR.

My first girlfriend used to use this excuse.

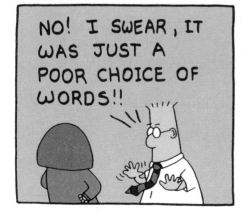

69 A lot of readers didn't get this one. Hint: which = witch.

. . . and His Ego

I imagine an ego looks like this. It's a cross between a brain and a cloud.

My obsession with hair loss continues.

This is the sort of cartoon I draw when I'm not getting enough sleep.

UH-OH! DILBERT'S ESCAPED EGO HAS GROWN SINCE GETTING THAT TOUPEE

HO-HO, WHAT A NIGHT! I CRASHED A PARTY FOR FEMALE POLICE OFFICERS!

I GOT PHONE NUMBERS FROM TWELVE WOMEN!

© 1990 United Feature Syndicate, Inc.

11-17

9-1-1?

THEY MUST BE ROOM-MATES.

I couldn't figure out how to end this sequence...

DILBERT CONFRONTS HIS OWN EGO

YOU CAN'T LEAVE ME NOW...

© 1990 United Feature Syndicate, Inc.

11-19

NOBODY TELLS ME WHAT TO DO! I AM PURE EGO FORCE! HA HA HA HA HA HA HA HA HA HA HA!!

MAYBE YOU'D LIKE TO DIS-CUSS THAT WITH MY INSECURITIES.

... It just kept getting stranger.

DILBERT'S EGO VS. HIS INSECURITIES

EGO →

C'MON, YOU COWARD!!

© 1990 United Feature Syndicate, Inc.

YOU MAY BE BIG, BUT I'M GOING TO POUND YOU INTO PUDDING!!

I'M GOING TO FAINT.

I DON'T THINK THIS WILL BE A CHILDREN'S FABLE ANYTIME SOON.

11-20

There!

I ended this one quickly.

. . . Dies

I killed Dilbert because sales to newspapers were slow. I thought this would shake things up. I don't think anyone noticed.

I want to be stuffed when I die.

YIKES! DILBERT'S INVENTION IS ALIVE !!

FLASH!

I AM A HOLOGRAPHIC RECORDING OF THE LATE DILBERT, WITH A MESSAGE TO DOGBERT FROM BEYOND THE GRAVE.

...AND MY RECIPE FOR CHILE CON CARNE IS AS FOLLOWS...

10-1

He's so cute with his ears up.

UGH...GOSH, WHAT A NIGHTMARE.

BOB, I JUST DREAMED DILBERT WAS KILLED BY DEER, AND ALL HE LEFT ME WAS HIS RECIPE FOR CHILE CON CARNE.

BAD NEWS...

HE'S REALLY DEAD ?

AND HIS CHILE CON CARNE STINKS.

10-2

My bid for reader sympathy failed. I decided to bring Dilbert back.

PLEASE, MISTER GARBAGE MAN, HELP US FIX DILBERT'S CLONING DEVICE AND BRING HIM BACK TO LIFE !!

THIS SHOULDN'T BE TOO HARD... STANDARD ANTI-LIGHT RESONANCE FILTERS... YEAH, I THINK I HAVE PARTS IN THE TRUCK.

10-4

YOU'RE GOING TO CLONE HIM FROM HIS OWN GARBAGE ?

DON'T TELL ANYBODY-- THERE MIGHT BE A STIGMA.

Is anti-light the same as dark ?

HI...UH, WHY AM I NAKED AND SITTING IN A GARBAGE CAN?

EITHER YOU WERE KILLED BY WILD DEER AND WE CLONED YOU BACK TO LIFE FROM YOUR OLD GARBAGE ... OR ...

I HOPE I LIKE THE SECOND CHOICE.

...OR YOU SAVED A LOT OF MONEY ON AN ABOVE-GROUND POOL.

... Travels

I was tired of this series, but it needed a conclusion.

I'M SORRY, SIR, BUT YOU'VE BEEN "BUMPED."

WHAT?!

HAPPY AIRLINE

I'VE GOT A TICKET! I DEMAND SATISFACTION! I'LL CALL THE PRESIDENT OF YOUR STUPID COMPANY!!

I WONDER IF THERE'S REALLY SUCH A THING AS THE "DUCT TAPE SECTION."

It seems as if I always get the worst seat.

WE'RE ALIVE... WE MUST HAVE BEEN THROWN CLEAR WHEN THE JET HIT THE MOUNTAIN

I'M CAPTAIN BOB. SORRY ABOUT THE CRASH. WHAT ARE THE ODDS I'D HIT THIS SAME MOUNTAIN ON EVERY FLIGHT?

WE'RE IN LUCK. CAPTAIN BOB KNOWS HOW TO SURVIVE THESE SITUATIONS.

NICE FOLKS. I'LL EAT THEM LAST.

I got complaints from people who don't think cannibal jokes are funny.

I'VE SURVIVED SEVERAL JET CRASHES THIS YEAR, SO LISTEN TO ME.

THE BEST WAY TO PREVENT FROSTBITE IS TO RUB WORCESTERSHIRE SAUCE ON YOUR BODY AND WHACK YOURSELF REPEATEDLY WITH A MEAT TENDERIZER.

I WONDER WHY HE HAD ENOUGH OF THESE FOR EVERYBODY?

WHACK WHACK

. . . Attempts to Join the Consumer Society

WELCOME TO ELECTRODE HUT. I'M HALF YOUR AGE, AND I KNOW MORE ABOUT ELECTRONICS THAN YOU EVER WILL. MAY I HELP YOU?

YES. I WOULD LIKE A HALF-DOZEN NIAD PULSE CONVERTERS AND AN ANZA BRUSH.

OR AM I BLUFFING?

THIS GUY IS GOOD.

In case you wondered, there's no such things as NIAD Pulse converters or ANZA Brushes.

I'M LOOKING FOR A FINE WOOL SUIT, IN THE $700 RANGE. SOMETHING FASHIONABLE YET TIMELESS.

TRY THIS $35 NYLON BEAUTY, SUITABLE FOR SWIMMING OR DINING OUT. THE BELL BOTTOMS ARE NO EXTRA CHARGE.

WOW!

I GUESS I WAS JUST BORN TO BE A FASHION PIONEER.

My pet peeve is that Salespeople always steer me to the cheapest items.

75

My first job was as a bank teller.

I love tools, even though I don't use them.

Women don't understand.

I CANNOT ALLOW THIS WITHDRAWAL...

BANK OF ETHEL

© 1990 United Feature Syndicate, Inc.

UNLESS YOU DEFEAT ME IN HAND TO HAND COMBAT.

THEY SEEM PRETTY SERIOUS ABOUT ENCOURAGING THE USE OF THEIR AUTOMATED TELLER MACHINES.

When I was a bank teller, I was robbed twice at gunpoint. I fantasized about beating up customers.

I HATE SHOPPING.

SALE

THERE'S NEVER A SALESPERSON WHEN YOU WANT TO BUY SOMETHING.

© 1991 United Feature Syndicate, Inc.

BUT WHEN YOU'RE JUST LOOKING...

I'm a shy shopper. I don't like to be a burden to the salespeople so I always say, "Just looking."

THIS SONY SNIFFMAN MAKES A NICE GIFT.

© 1991 United Feature Syndicate, Inc.

YOU CAN PLAY THE SMELLS OF YOUR FAVORITE STARS!

TRY IT— IT'S DONNY OSMOND'S GYM BAG.

IS IT "NEW DONNY" OR CLASSIC?

If this existed, someone would buy it.

It's funny to me that I have to prove to the bank that I'm honest.

When I was a kid, my grandmother convinced me that brown eggs were tastier. Now I just wonder what route they took through the hen.

This might actually work someday.

CAN YOU HELP ME?

NO, I'M AFRAID I CAN'T.

YOU SEE, I GET PAID THE SAME LOW HOURLY WAGE WHETHER YOU BUY THAT SHIRT OR NOT. AND AFTER YEARS IN THIS BUSINESS I'VE LEARNED TO DESPISE THE GENERAL PUBLIC.

PLEASE... I HAVE EXACT CHANGE.

I HAVE NO WAY OF KNOWING IF THAT'S TRUE

I believe all salespeople hate me. If they didn't before, they do now.

I'M GOING TO THE BIG TECHNOLOGY SHOW.

WHAT DO YOU DO THERE?

I WILL WADE THROUGH A VAST SEA OF MOSTLY CURLY-HAIRED GUYS WITH FACIAL HAIR AND GLASSES. AND I WILL LOOK AT THOUSANDS OF INDISTINCT PRODUCTS.

IT'S LIKE SALMON RETURNING TO ITS BIRTHPLACE.

BUT WITHOUT THE SPAWNING OPPORTUNITIES.

Why do so many technology people have curly hair and glasses?

AT THE TRADE SHOW...

UH-OH. A VENDOR IS SCANNING ME.

I'M CAUGHT IN A TRACTOR BEAM! RED ALERT! RED ALERT!

LOSING LIFE SUPPORT SYSTEMS...

ZZZZ

... AND IT CAN EVEN CALCULATE FRACTIONS!

All vendor demos are boring. It's the law, I think.

UH...EXCUSE ME, EARTH DOG.

WE HAVE TRAVELED FROM A DISTANT PLANET TO FIND OUT WHY EARTH DOGS ARE FORCED TO EAT FROM DIRTY LITTLE BOWLS WHILE HUMANS USE PLATES.

WELL, BASICALLY, IT'S POLITICAL. IT ALL BEGAN AFTER THE UNSUCCESSFUL POODLE REBELLION IN FRANCE, AROUND 1723...

BETTER USE A PENCIL...

S. Adams 5-8   © 1989 United Feature Syndicate, Inc.

I support equal rights for pets.

I'VE DECIDED TO MAKE SOME DOG FRIENDS, BUT I DON'T EVEN KNOW WHAT OTHER DOGS DO WHEN THEY GET TOGETHER.

WELL, I SUPPOSE THEY WOULD BARK LIKE IDIOTS, RUN AROUND IN CIRCLES, AND SNIFF EVERY PART OF YOUR BODY.

© 1989 United Feature Syndicate, Inc.

I GUESS "SCRABBLE" IS OUT OF THE QUESTION.

S. Adams 5-16

In the beginning, Dogbert still had traces of dog-like behavior.

I'M HAVING NIGHT-MARES. MOVE OVER.

JUST DON'T HOG ALL THE COVERS.

© 1989 United Feature Syndicate, Inc.

AT LEAST GIVE ME MY PAJAMA TOP...

SHHH...

7-29   S. Adams

My cat does this. ♪

DOGBERT

My personal experience with dogs was primarily with a beagle named Lucy, our family dog for most of my childhood. Lucy never once came when I called—not once in fourteen years. In fact, she did absolutely nothing except what she wanted to do. If I tried to pet her she would growl, grab my shirt by the cuff, rip the entire sleeve off, and run down the hall with it like a trophy. (That actually happened.) It was quite obvious that my family was subservient to the dog. Lucy slept on any furniture she wanted, she came and went as she pleased, never wore a leash, and had food and water served at her discretion.

Dogbert took on a bit of Lucy, particularly the beagle ears, round body, and attitude. He also took on a bit of the dark side of my own personality, the part that wants to conquer the planet and make all the people my personal servants.

Dogbert gets to say all the things that I might be thinking but can't say for fear of retribution. His view is that the entire world and all the people in it are here for his personal entertainment.

There's no explanation of why Dogbert chooses to live with Dilbert, except that he finds him amusing. Once in a great while we'll see some glimpses of affection. And if Dilbert gets in deep trouble we can count on Dogbert to bail him out.

81

Dogbert was more of a pet in the first year. He wasn't obedient, but he *was* a pet.

Dogbert is starting to show his true personality now.

I don't remember why I thought Dogbert should be egg-shaped.

I can't imagine putting Dogbert in a leash now.

Dogbert shows emotion with fur, eyebrows, and ears.

HEY, DOGBERT, YOU WANT TO GO CAMPING THIS WEEKEND?

WHY DON'T WE JUST SLEEP IN THE GARAGE, EAT BUGS AND NOT TAKE SHOWERS.

9-22

© 1989 United Feature Syndicate, Inc.

THAT IS COMPLETELY DIFFERENT FROM CAMPING, FOR REASONS WHICH WILL COME TO ME.

BECAUSE WE MIGHT NOT GET LOST?

This is my view of "roughing it," as expressed by Dogbert.

I'M SORRY, BUT IT SEEMS YOU'VE FAILED THE WRITTEN PORTION OF THE DOG LICENSE TEST.

IMPOSSIBLE!

FOR EXAMPLE, THIS QUESTION ON "NATURAL ENEMIES": THE CORRECT ANSWER IS "MAILMAN." YOU WROTE-IN "FAX MACHINE."

© 1990 United Feature Syndicate, Inc.

HOW'D IT GO?

THE "DEPARTMENT OF DOGS" DOES NOT KEEP UP WITH EMERGING TRENDS.

1-12

Here I was still playing with dog stereotypes. No dogs complained.

YOU'VE HEARD THE "OTHER" TIRE COMPANY IMPLY THAT YOUR CHILD'S SAFETY DEPENDS ON ITS PRODUCT...

THAT'S NOTHING. IF YOU DON'T BUY OUR TIRES YOUR WHOLE STINKIN' EXTENDED FAMILY WILL CROAK!!!

© 1990 United Feature Syndicate, Inc.

AND DON'T GET TOO ATTACHED TO THE FAMILY DOG, EITHER. HA HA HA HA HA!!

2-10

He's too cute when his ears fly up.

85

... SO TO DO OUR PART FOR EAST-WEST RELATIONS...

I'VE DECIDED TO HOST A DOG FROM THE SOVIET EXCHANGE PROGRAM.

WHAT?

DOGBERT, I'D LIKE YOU TO MEET NIKITA... NIKITA DORGACHEV.

CHARMED.

Dogbert begins to get political. Or maybe it was just an excuse to show what dogs look like with hats.

YOU SEE, DORGY, UNDER OUR CAPITALIST SYSTEM ANYBODY CAN BECOME RICH.

HOW?

INHERITANCE AND CRIME ARE THE MOST POPULAR METHODS.

WHICH IS PREFERRED METHOD?

IT'S BEST TO HAVE YOUR PARENTS DO THE CRIME AND LET YOU INHERIT IT.

Have you ever noticed how many wealthy industrialists started out by doing illegal things? I'd love to see some statistics on that. And more dogs with hats.

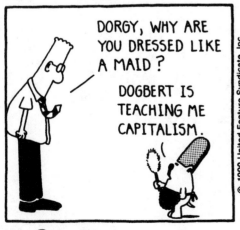

DORGY, WHY ARE YOU DRESSED LIKE A MAID?

DOGBERT IS TEACHING ME CAPITALISM.

TODAY I AM LOWLY MAID. BUT WITH HARD WORK I WILL BE PROMOTED TO JOB AS MAJOR INDUSTRIALIST.

RIGHT?

APPARENTLY THERE IS FLAW IN SYSTEM.

YEAH, BUT WE BLAME IT ON THE JAPANESE.

Personally, I love capitalism, but it's a great subject for humor because it  creates losers more often than winners. (I've been both.)

THIS IS SO NICE...
JUST A MAN AND
HIS MUTT OUT FOR
A WALK.

"MUTT"?!

I THINK OF IT MORE AS A
"CANINE AND A CLOD" OR
A "DOG AND A DUMMY"...
MAYBE A "POOCH AND A
PINHEAD" OR A "BOWSER
AND A BLOCKHEAD."

I THINK THAT'S
ENOUGH.

A "HOUND AND
A HINEY."

If a human had spoken the word "hiney," I probably wouldn't have gotten away with it.

DOGBERT, I HAVE
COME FOR YOU.

YOW!

WAIT WAIT!
DON'T I GET TO
CHALLENGE YOU
TO SOME CONTEST
TO PLAY FOR
MY LIFE!!?

OKAY... I THROW
THIS FRISBEE —
YOU TRY TO CATCH
IT IN YOUR
MOUTH.

DID YOU HAVE
ANYTHING
MORE DE-
GRADING?

I always feel sorry for dogs who catch "Frisbees." It looks humiliating.

FREEZE!!!
I'M A DOG
CATCHER!

WHAT, NO COLLAR?
YOU'RE GOING TO
THE PUPPY PENI-
TENTIARY, PAL!

YOUR HUMAN
TURNED
YOU IN?

HE DIDN'T
THINK A PIT
BULL SHOULD
WEAR HIS
HAIR THIS
WAY.

This might be the world's first gay dog cartoon.

Dogbert continues to get more assertive and clever.

Debris is hard to draw.

It _would_ explain everything.

I'VE DECIDED TO JOIN THE ANTI-FUR MOVEMENT.

ISN'T THAT HYPOCRITICAL? YOU WEAR A FUR COAT EVERYDAY.

OH...YEAH, NEVER MIND...

WAIT...

Most issues are not black and white. I'm suspicious of anyone who has a firm belief about anything.

WE CAN SPEND THE FIRST DAY AT CLYDE CANYON HIKING AND EXPLORING...

RRRR

ARE YOU STILL MAD ABOUT THE FLIGHT ARRANGEMENTS?

SIR, YOU'LL HAVE TO STORE YOUR CARRY-ON LUGGAGE IN THE OVERHEAD COMPARTMENT.

RRRR...

This is another reason Dogbert doesn't respect humans. He wouldn't put up with this now.

AH... A FULL WEEK OF HIKING AND EXPLORING.

CLYDE CANYON TRAIL

CLYDE CANYON

WE'RE GONNA BE PRETTY TIRED OF THIS PLACE BY THE END OF THE WEEK.

To me, all vacations look like this — a long hike to something that <u>89→</u> looks better in the brochure.

AFTER ONE WEEK OF CAMPING

THIS VACATION TO CLYDE CANYON HAS BEEN A MAJOR RIP-OFF.

I'M GLAD IT'S OVER.

WHY ARE YOU TWO IN THAT HOLE WHEN BEAUTIFUL CLYDE CANYON IS JUST OVER THE RIDGE?

MAYBE WE SHOULDN'T BOTHER GETTING OUR PHOTOS DEVELOPED.

There's an art to taking vacations — an art I'm not good at. I always think I must be doing something wrong.

AS MY DOG, I THINK YOU SHOULD BE DOING MORE TO HELP ME MEET ATTRACTIVE SINGLE WOMEN DURING OUR WALKS.

TRY TO BE CUTER, AND LOOK MORE PET-ABLE.

AND IT'S NOT FUNNY WHEN YOU DO YOUR IMPRESSION OF A FROTHING MAD DOG EVERY TIME SOMEBODY WALKS BY.

THAT'S MY JOHN SUNUNU IMPRESSION.

Dogbert's joy of taunting Dilbert is getting more developed now.

DOGBERT, I GOT TINY "PCS" PHONES FOR BOTH OF US.

IT'S THE NEWEST TECHNOLOGY! I'LL BE ABLE TO CALL YOU AT ANY TIME, NO MATTER WHERE WE ARE!

PCS = Personal Communications Services

WHY MUST ALL PROGRESS START OUT AS SOMETHING ANNOYING?

Bzzz Bzzz Bzzz

I wrote this in 1991. This month is the first time you can **90** get a PCS phone in my area.

I had a big green pillow like this. It was great for watching TV on the floor.

DILBERT
By Scott Adams

DOGBERT, COME LOOK AT OUR NEW CAR!

IT HAS ALL OF THE MOST IMPORTANT SAFETY FEATURES.

YOU GOT YOUR ANTI-LOCK BRAKES, YOUR REINFORCED BUMPERS, YOUR AUTOMATIC SEATBELTS AND YOUR DRIVER-SIDE AIR BAG.

I DIDN'T HEAR "PASSENGER SIDE AIR BAG" IN THAT LIST

IT TURNS OUT THAT IT'S ONLY ECONOMICAL TO SAVE THE PERSON WHO MAKES THE BUYING DECISION.

4-19

BUT I GOT A BABY SEAT IN CASE YOU WANT TO USE THAT.

WELL, THANK YOU FOR LETTING ME CHOOSE BETWEEN HUMILIATION AND DEATH.

I'VE GOT A BETTER IDEA.

OOH... JUST WAIT UNTIL MY TURN.

WATCH ME RAM THAT COP CAR.

© 1992 United Feature Syndicate, Inc.

My girlfriend complained about the lack of an airbag on her side.

91

HOW WAS YOUR DAY, DOGBERT?

HEY! WHAT'S THAT SMELL?

JUST AS I SUSPECTED — YOU STOPPED TO PET THE NEIGHBOR'S CAT!

IT MEANT NOTHING. IT WAS MORE OF A PAT THAN A PET.

SAVE YOUR LIES FOR THE TRIAL.

In small ways, I revealed that Dilbert and Dogbert liked each other.

I'M AN ATTORNEY FOR MISTER DOGBERT...

HE'S SUING YOU FOR "PETIMONY." YOU ALLEGEDLY PET THE NEIGHBOR'S CAT...

SEE... IT WAS A PAT, NOT A PET. LIKE THIS...

OH LOOK, IT'S "GARFIELD," YOUR FAVORITE...

. . . Reveals His Sarcasm

I THOUGHT I HAD THIS TUXEDO THING FIGURED OUT. BUT WHAT THE HECK IS THIS?

OH, THAT'S THE KUMBER-BUZLE. YOU WEAR IT ON YOUR HEAD LIKE A SWEATBAND.

THEN YOU CLIP YOUR PENS AND PENCILS TO THE KUMBERBUZLE.

AH, THAT EXPLAINS WHY THE SHIRT HAS NO POCKET.

If you ask me, Tuxedos have too many unnecessary parts.

92

CHAPTER IV. "TIME MANAGEMENT"

"ALWAYS POSTPONE MEETINGS WITH TIME-WASTING MORONS."

HOW DO YOU DO THAT?

CAN I GET BACK TO YOU ON THAT?

5-10

The art of time management is really the ability to blow people off without guilt.

DO YOU REALIZE THAT IF WE STAY TOGETHER FOR SEVEN YEARS, WE ARE CONSIDERED MARRIED BY COMMON LAW?

THAT MEANS I OWN HALF OF ALL YOUR WORLDLY POSSESSIONS.

5-12

I PLAN TO SELL MY HALF... MAYBE BUY SOME TASTEFUL THINGS INSTEAD.

Here's a glimpse of Dogbert's growth into more human preferences.

RRRR

POW!

S.Adams 5-18

REGRETTABLY, YOU VIOLATED MY AIR SPACE.

These would be fun toys.

EXPERTS SAY THAT WHEN YOU HAVE MASTERED THE MENTAL GAME, THE BALL WILL APPEAR TO GROW LARGER.

OKAY, BUT I STILL THINK THESE BALLS ARE NOT REGULATION SIZE.

PROBABLY JUST A REFLECTION OF YOUR LACK OF CONFIDENCE.

THREE MOTH BALLS AND A GOOD STORY ARE MORE EFFECTIVE THAN YEARS OF LESSONS.

© 1989 United Feature Syndicate, Inc.

S. Adams 6-17

Dogbert increasingly comes out on top by having no ethical limitations.

...AND NATURE HAS A WAY OF COMPENSATING FOR WEAKNESSES.

REALLY?

THAT'S WHY BLIND PEOPLE OFTEN DEVELOP GREAT HEARING.

S. Adams

I GUESS THAT ALSO EXPLAINS WHY STUPID PEOPLE HAVE BIG MOUTHS.

© 1989 United Feature Syndicate, Inc.

7-10

My cat sits on my legs like that.

WHOA! LOOKS LIKE WE GOT A PIPPIN HAWK, A PRICKLY BEAK MUD SWALLOW, AND A BALD EAGLE.

ROBIN.

HOW IS IT THAT YOU HAVE SPOTTED 1,700 EXOTIC BIRDS THIS MORNING, AND ALL I HAVE SEEN IS ONE ROBIN?

S. Adams 9-12

© 1989 United Feature Syndicate, Inc.

LOOK! A MONKEY-FACED DISCO HAWK!!

WHERE?!

I have a friend who was a bird watcher. They're very competitive.

IF I DIED TOMORROW, WHAT WOULD YOU WRITE ON MY TOMBSTONE?

I ALWAYS ASSUMED THERE WOULD BE NO TOMBSTONE.

AH...YOU WOULD HAVE ME CREMATED.

OR STUFFED, WHICHEVER IS CHEAPER.

In 1989, I only owned one piece of new furniture. It was the green recliner chair Dogbert is in.

QUICK, QUICK! GIVE ME YOUR HAND!!!

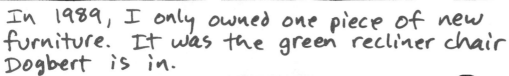

AAACHOOO

THANKS... I ALWAYS PUT A HAND OVER MY MOUTH WHEN I SNEEZE.

My cat sneezes on me intentionally.

I CAN FEEL THE STATIC ELECTRICITY BUILDING...

SHUFFLE SHUFFLE

SHUFFLE SHUFFLE

SHUFFLE SHUFFLE

SHUFFLE SHUFFLE

I MOST CERTAINLY WILL **NOT** CALL YOU "THOR, DOG OF THUNDER."

PREPARE TO DIE.

Thor was one of my favorite comics as a kid.

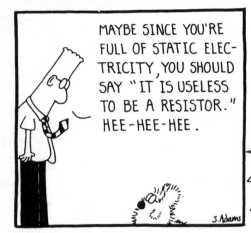

A lot of people don't have the capacitor for appreciating nerd puns.

I was a contestant on "Wheel of Fortune"... and lost.

why don't dogs get cavities? What's up with that?

WELL, MR. DOGBERT, WHAT COULD I DO TO CONVINCE YOU TO PUT YOUR NEW WEALTH IN OUR BANK?

STRETCH YOUR POLYESTER PANTS OVER THE TOP OF YOUR HEAD.

I HOPE MONEY DOESN'T CHANGE ME.

When I worked in a bank, we <u>hated</u> the rich customers.

KNOWLEDGE IS POWER, DOGBERT.

SOMEDAY, THE PEOPLE WHO KNOW HOW TO USE COMPUTERS WILL RULE OVER THOSE WHO DON'T.

AND THEY WILL HAVE A SPECIAL NAME FOR US.

SECRETARIES.

I had a neighbor who believed that computer skills would lead to nothing but clerical opportunities, because the computers would do the rest.

DID ANYBODY CALL ON YOUR NEW VIDEO PHONE YET?

NO.

DON'T YOU THINK THAT THE ONLY PEOPLE WHO WILL BUY VIDEO PHONES ARE MALE TECHIE DWEEBS LIKE YOU?

THEREFORE, WOULDN'T IT BE CHEAPER TO BUY A MIRROR?

IT'S HELL BEING AN EARLY ADOPTER.

I think this about

97 Internet "chats" too.

GET IT, DOGBERT!

BLAM!

MAYBE I SHOULD JUST GET A CAT.

GOOD IDEA, BUT THEY'RE HARDER TO THROW.

Dogbert's views on the "Frisbee" concept are becoming clearer.

OUR SCHOOL SYSTEM IS A COMPLETE FAILURE, DOGBERT.

WHY'S THAT?

THE SCHOOLS SHOULD BE PREPARING THESE KIDS TO BE SCIENTISTS AND ENGINEERS. THAT'S THE ONLY WAY OUR ECONOMY WILL PROSPER.

INSTEAD, WE'LL BE A NATION OF MAIDS AND JANITORS.

YEAH, BUT THINK HOW CLEAN IT WILL BE.

I think every story has a positive side. But I got complaints from maids and janitors after this ran.

I CAN'T WAIT TO GROW UP AND GET OUT OF SCHOOL.

ACTUALLY, NORIKO, YOUR GENERATION WILL HAVE TO TAKE CLASSES AND WORK FULL-TIME YOUR WHOLE LIVES ... ASSUMING ANY JOBS EXIST.

BUT ON THE PLUS SIDE, TELEVISION WILL HAVE A THOUSAND CHANNELS.

THAT'S IT; SOMEBODY'S GOT SOME EXPLAINING TO DO!

Noriko is my girlfriend's middle name. This character is based on a kindergarten → 98 → picture of her I saw.

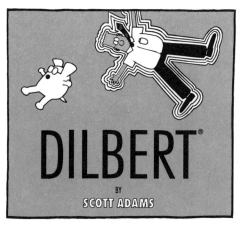

A SMALL BAND OF THE CREATURES WERE KNOWN TO LIVE HIGH IN AN ARTIFICIAL STRUCTURE.

ON MY WAY TO STUDY THEM I TOOK NOTE OF THE NATIVE VEGETATION.

RENTED

THE YOUNGER MALES WERE AT PLAY. THEY BECAME SELF-CONSCIOUS WHEN WATCHED.

THE DOMINANT MALE HAD A GRAY BACK. HE CONTROLLED THE OTHERS BY WAVING LITTLE ENVELOPES.

THERE WERE FEW FEMALES IN THE GROUP. THE LESS DOMINANT MALES HAD NO CHANCE OF MATING.

UNLIKE OTHER SPECIES THEY HAD NO INSTINCT FOR GROOMING.

WANT TO GROOM?

DROP DEAD.

MY TIME WAS UP. BUT I WILL MISS THEM, THOSE...

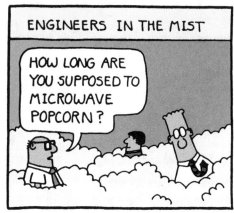

ENGINEERS IN THE MIST

HOW LONG ARE YOU SUPPOSED TO MICROWAVE POPCORN?

I felt like an observer in the land of engineers at Pacific Bell. I wasn't an engineer by training, but I worked closely with them.

I RECENTLY RECEIVED THIS ANGRY LETTER FROM A MISTER "DORK."

MR. DORK INFORMS ME THAT THE MANY PEOPLE SURNAMED DORK ARE NOT AMUSED THAT I ONCE USED THE WORD "DORKAGE." HE DEMANDS AN APOLOGY.

I APOLOGIZE TO ALL THE DORKS WHO WERE OFFENDED. I HOPE WE CAN PUT THIS BEHIND US.

Sometimes Dogbert speaks for me.

. . . the Many Occupations

THE DESIGNS FOR MY REVOLUTIONARY NEW "HOME DEFENSE SYSTEM" ARE NOW COMPLETE.

WELL, THIS IS VERY DETAILED. BUT WHERE DO YOU THINK WE CAN FIND THIS MANY "FLYING ATTACK PORCUPINES?"

JUST TRY TO GET A COMPLIMENT OUT OF THAT MAN.

My best ideas are the ones that people hate the most.

ARE YOU REALLY GOING THROUGH WITH THE UNAUTHORIZED BIOGRAPHY OF ME?

YES.

I'M UP TO THE PART WHERE JACKIE "O" AND LIZ TAYLOR FIGHT A DUEL FOR YOUR LOVE.

TRAGICALLY, NEITHER ARE AWARE THAT YOU'RE CARRYING STEVE GARVEY'S BABY!

TAP TAP TAP

Dogbert used a "Macintosh" in those days.

DAY ONE AS A SUBSTITUTE TEACHER

JENNIFER! PUT THAT FLAME-THROWER AWAY RIGHT THIS MINUTE!

EUGENE! RELEASE THOSE HOSTAGES OR I SHALL BE FORCED TO FLING THIS CHALK ERASER AT YOUR HEAD!

S.Adams 1-17

IS THAT A "STINGER" MISSILE LAUNCHER? WELL, I HOPE YOU BROUGHT ENOUGH FOR EVERYBODY!

I DID.

Dogbert is perfect for exploring the downsides of other occupations because he brings a surreal element to surreal situations.

OKAY, CLASS . . . PUT YOUR WEAPONS AWAY AND OPEN YOUR TV GUIDES.

TIMMY, PLEASE READ ALOUD THE PASSAGE FROM "FALCON CREST" UNDER THE FRIDAY LISTINGS.

1-18

THERE'S GOT TO BE A BETTER WAY TO TEACH SEX EDUCATION.

S.Adams

I'VE DECIDED TO BECOME AN AMBUSH REPORTER, LIKE MIKE WALLACE.

NEWS

IS IT TRUE YOU MADE ALL OF YOUR MONEY UNETHICALLY AND YOU'RE HAVING AN AFFAIR?

S.Adams 5-14

YES!! YES!! HOW DID YOU FIND ME?!

YOU WERE CHOSEN RANDOMLY.

JUST A MOMENT, LITTLE GIRL. I'M DOGBERT, THE AMBUSH REPORTER.

IS IT TRUE THAT YOU PRETEND TO BE CUTE IN ORDER TO MANIPULATE ADULTS!!

OH, HEY, WAIT... I'M JUST KIDDING. CAN I BUY YOU SOMETHING EXPENSIVE?

SNIFF SNIFF

WELCOME TO DOGBERT'S SCHOOL FOR ASPIRING SELF-SERVICE GAS STATION ATTENDANTS.

I WILL TEACH YOU HOW TO SIT IN A LITTLE BUILDING AND DO NOTHING.

THESE SAME SKILLS CAN BE TRANSFERRED TO A CAREER IN CONGRESS OR FOTOMAT.

REALLY? FOTOMAT?!

There actually are schools for self-service gas station attendants. You probably fail if you try to pump gas.

I HEARD YOU CLOSED YOUR SCHOOL FOR SELF-SERVICE GAS STATION ATTENDANTS.

IT DIDN'T WORK OUT.

I WAS TEACHING THE SECTION ON REFOLDING MAPS... FRUSTRATIONS WERE HIGH... AT FIRST, THE PAPER CUTS WERE MINOR, BUT PANIC SWEPT THE ROOM.

WELL, HOW BAD COULD...

THEY'RE ALL DEAD...

I wanted to end this series, so I killed all the extras.

I GOT A JOB AS A USED CAR SALES-MAN.

DOES IT PAY WELL?

I'M NOT IN IT FOR THE MONEY. I JUST ENJOY LYING TO STRANGERS.

THIS ONE WAS OWNED BY CARLOS THE DIAMOND SMUGGLER. IT CORNERS WELL, BUT THE GAS MILEAGE IS BAD -- ALMOST AS IF IT HAS WEIGHTS HIDDEN IN THE DOOR PANELS.

Dogbert would be the perfect used car salesman.

MISTER DOGBERT, THE TOBACCO LOBBY IS VERY INTERESTED IN BUYING YOUR SENATOR.

WE'VE BEEN TAKING A BEATING FROM THE ANTI-SMOKING FASCISTS. I BLAME THE MEDIA.

WHAT WE NEED IS MORE ATTENTION ON THE POSITIVE ASPECTS OF SMOKING ... LIKE SEX APPEAL.

YES, SIR.

The spokespeople for tobacco companies always look half dead. The Surgeon General should make them put their pictures on every pack.

MISTER PRESIDENT, THERE'S ANOTHER OPENING ON THE SUPREME COURT. ONE OF THE OLD GUYS WANDERED AWAY.

I RECOMMEND NOMINATING A DOG THIS TIME. THEY TEND TO BE LOYAL AND EVERYBODY LIKES THEM.

IT'S FOR YOU... GEORGE SOME-BODY.

TAKE A MESSAGE.

I can't draw caricatures, so I hide them behind chairs if they're 103 real people.

DOGBERT'S SUPREME COURT NOMINATION HEARINGS

DO YOU HAVE ANY OPINIONS ON THE RIGHT TO PRIVACY?

NO. IN FACT, I'VE NEVER FORMED AN IMPORTANT OPINION IN MY ENTIRE LIFE.

YOU MUST THINK WE'RE IDIOTS.

OKAY, I'VE FORMED ONE OPINION... BUT THAT'S ALL.

This was during the Clarence Thomas senate confirmation process.

AS YOUR CONSULTANT, I RECOMMEND THE "CAN-O-MATIC" TO REDUCE STAFF LEVELS.

DISGUISED AS A RESTROOM STALL, THE CAN-O-MATIC RANDOMLY FIRES PEOPLE BY SLAPPING A PINK SLIP ON THEIR BACKS AND CATAPULTING THEM OUT OF THE BUILDING.

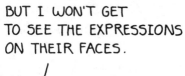

BUT I WON'T GET TO SEE THE EXPRESSIONS ON THEIR FACES.

WELL, WE COULD FLING THEM PAST THE SECURITY CAMERAS HERE...

Dogbert ventures into the consulting field. He'll be there a lot.

DOGBERT'S SCHOOL OF COMMON SENSE.

TODD, SHOW THE CLASS HOW YOU HAND THESE SCISSORS TO RUSSELL.

DON'T RUN! DON'T RUN!

AAAGH!

SORRY, RUSSELL. IT'S THE TEACHER'S FAULT; HE DIDN'T EVEN ASK IF I NEED LEFT-HANDED SCISSORS.

↖ sometimes spelled "AAARGH!"

DILBERT

By Scott Adams

THANKS FOR AGREEING TO BABY-SIT, DOGBERT.

NO SWEAT.

DOGGIE-BERT!

SIT DOWN, BRET.

YOU'RE IN YOUR MOST INNOCENT AND IMPRESSIONABLE YEARS.

AS AN ADULT, IT IS MY DUTY TO FILL YOUR SPONGE-LIKE BRAIN WITH INCREDIBLE NONSENSE FOR MY OWN ENTERTAINMENT.

YOUR PARENTS ARE REALLY SPACE ALIENS.

1-5-92

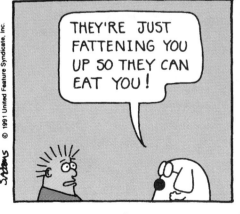

THEY'RE JUST FATTENING YOU UP SO THEY CAN EAT YOU!

THE SLAUGHTER-HOUSE IS A PLACE THEY CALL KINDERGARTEN!!

THANKS, DOGBERT. DID YOU CHANGE HIM?

PROBABLY.

My babies look like old men.

105

I tend to think communication causes more problems than it solves.

If you don't work for a big company, you don't know how accurate the dialogue is.

I'LL BE REPRESENTING YOU CORPORATE EMPLOYEES IN A CLASS ACTION SUIT. YOUR COMPANY HAS SUCKED THE LIFE FORCE OUT OF YOU AND TURNED YOU INTO LITTLE RAGS.

MY FEE WILL BE ON A CONTINGENCY BASIS. THAT MEANS I GET THE ENTIRE SETTLEMENT PLUS I'LL USE YOU TO WAX MY BMW.

7-20

I'VE FOUND THE PERFECT CLIENTS.

SOUNDS FAIR.

DON'T MAKE WAVES.

When I worked in a cubicle, I felt like a little rag.

I PLAN TO USE MY NEW WEALTH TO BUILD AN AMUSEMENT PARK.

DOGBERTLAND WILL HAVE THRILLING RIDES LIKE "THE WEDGIE" AND I'LL HAVE A MAZE IN FRONT OF THE RESTROOMS.

4-23

THE CUSTOMERS WILL HATE THIS.

IF THEY WANT FUN THEY CAN BUILD THEIR OWN PARK.

The more selfish and mean that Dogbert is, the funnier he is.

I'M GOING TO START MY OWN BOOK PUBLISHING COMPANY SO I CAN REJECT PEOPLE ALL DAY LONG.

6-27

I'LL DISMISS THEIR LIFE'S WORK WITH A GESTURE AND A WITTY COMMENT.

BOTTOM LINE, I'M JUST NOT A PEOPLE PERSON.

I'VE NOTICED.

People tell me they like it when Dogbert wags.

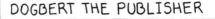

DOGBERT THE PUBLISHER

DEAR TIM,
YOUR BOOK DOES NOT MEET OUR CURRENT PUBLISHING NEEDS.

YOUR PLOT WAS LAME AND I HATED YOUR CHARACTERS. AND BY ASSOCIATION I HAVE COME TO HATE YOU TOO.

FOR SAFETY REASONS, I HIRED AN ILLITERATE PERSON TO RIP UP YOUR MANUSCRIPT. I WOULD USE THE RETURN ENVELOPE YOU PROVIDED BUT I'M AFRAID YOU MIGHT HAVE LICKED THE STAMPS.

I knew a guy named Tim who was rudely turned down by a publisher.

WE'VE HIRED THE DOGBERT AD AGENCY TO GIVE OUR COMPANY A NEW IMAGE.

I USED A COMPUTER TO SUGGEST A NEW HI-TECH NAME FOR YOUR COMPANY. THE PROGRAM RANDOMLY COMBINES WORDS FROM ASTRONOMY AND ELEC-TRONICS.

THE FIRST CHOICE IS "URANUS-HERTZ"

I LIKE IT.

This was banned from at least one newspaper.

THE COMPANY HIRED AN ETHICS EXPERT TO HELP US THROUGH THE GRAY AREAS.

YOUR CALLS TO THE ETHICS OFFICE ARE COMPLETELY CONFIDENTIAL.

THANKS FOR SHARING THAT. I OWN YOU NOW, WEASEL-BOY.

Does anyone believe the concept of corporate confidentiality?

DOGBERT'S TECH SUPPORT

I THINK I KNOW WHAT YOUR PROBLEM IS...

TAKE ALL THE PARTS AND ARRANGE THEM IN NEAT PILES. NOW STAND ON YOUR CHAIR SO YOU CAN SEE ABOVE YOUR CUBICLE WALL...

NOW SHOUT "DOES ANY-BODY KNOW HOW TO READ A MANUAL?"

This was a big hit with tech support people. (They despise callers.)

AS NEW OWNER OF THIS COMPANY I HEREBY BAN ALL MEETINGS OVER ONE HOUR. THE DRESS CODE IS CASUAL. STATUS REPORTS ARE OPTIONAL!

NO MORE MISSION STATE-MENTS OR "VISIONS." OUR MOTTO IS "HAVE FUN, SATISFY CUSTOMERS, MAKE MONEY."

AND STOCK OPTIONS FOR ALL.

WE CAN FIT FIVE MORE IN THIS CUBICLE IF WE REMOVE THE CHAIR.

This is ↑ my motto.

WE'VE GOT A LOT OF EMPTY CUBICLES BECAUSE OF DOWNSIZING.

I HIRED THE DOGBERT CONSTRUCTION COMPANY TO CONVERT PART OF THE OFFICE INTO PRISON CELLS WHICH WE'LL LEASE TO THE STATE.

SOUNDS LIKE A BIG JOB.

NAH. A LITTLE PAINT, NEW CARPET AND WE'RE THERE.

It could happen.

Rush Limbaugh's fans attacked me for this. But Rush wasn't my target. I just thought it would be a good job for Dogbert.

People get mad when they think Dogbert's opinions are my opinions. Sometimes →110→ they are, but usually not.

WELCOME TO THE DOGBERT SHOW. TODAY I TALK ABOUT GETTING GOVERNMENT OFF OUR BACKS.

I DREAM OF A WORLD WHERE SOMEDAY YOU CAN BUY LIQUOR, CIGARETTES AND FIREARMS AT A DRIVE-THRU WINDOW AND USE THEM ALL BEFORE YOU GET HOME.

BASICALLY, ANYTHING THAT GETS RID OF PEOPLE IS OKAY WITH ME. BUT BEFORE YOU GO, BUY MY NEW BOOK...

Everybody got mad about that one.

. . . Schemes to Conquer the World

IMAGINE MY SURPRISE WHEN I SAW THIS AD FOR DOCTOR DOGBERT'S SEMINAR ON DEVELOPING SELF-CONFIDENCE. OKAY, WHAT'S THE SCAM?

I FIGURED THIS WOULD BE A GOOD WAY TO FIND A BUNCH OF MEEK PEOPLE TO DO MY BIDDING. IF THEY REFUSE, I'LL YELL AT THEM AND HURT THEIR LITTLE FEELINGS.

THEN I'LL LEVERAGE THAT POWER INTO VAST WEALTH OR MAYBE WORLD DOMINATION.

NO! BAD DOGGY!

© 1989 United Feature Syndicate, Inc.

Someday I expect Dogbert to conquer the world.

THERE... PERFECT.

WHAT'S THAT, DOGBERT?

I'VE CREATED THE VELCRO SHIRT POCKET! IT ATTACHES TO YOUR CHEST HAIRS WHILE SWIMMING OR SHOWERING.

HMM... MIGHT WORK.

YOU MAY ALSO BE INTERESTED IN MY NEW VELCRO CHEST HAIR.

I'm a wanna-be inventor. I'm still working on my perpetual motion  machine. Ironically, I can't seem to stop.

DILBERT®

By Scott Adams

DING DONG

I'LL GET THE DOOR.

GREETINGS, EARTHLING. WE ARE AN ADVANCED RACE FROM THE PLANET MOOTHRON.

WE CAME TO SHARE OUR SECRETS FOR ENDING HUNGER, POVERTY AND DISEASE.

WHAT'S IN IT FOR ME?

© 1989 United Feature Syndicate, Inc.

I'LL ALWAYS WONDER IF THERE WAS A BETTER WAY TO HANDLE THAT.

S. Adams 7-9

Imagine an advanced race of aliens who talk to the average human; Do you think they'll be impressed?

Jim Davis, the author of "Garfield" asked for the original of this. I traded for one of his. At the time, it was my biggest economic gain as a cartoonist.

This cartoon captures the Dogbert attitude better than any other.

Gorby jokes don't age well.

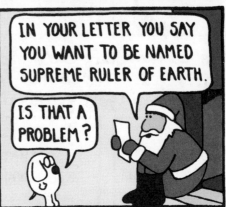

Wouldn't it be great to own an elf?

This plan could actually work.

I'M GOING TO FORM A PERSONALITY CULT TO HONOR ME.

I'LL TAKE EVERYBODY'S MONEY AND MAKE THEM WEAR BATHROBES WITH MY PICTURE ON THE BACK.

WOULDN'T IT BE CHEAPER TO BRAND THEM AND LET THEM RUN NAKED?

AS A RULE, WE'RE NOT TALKING ABOUT ATTRACTIVE PEOPLE HERE.

Do supermodels ever join cults? I don't think so.

I'M HOPING YOU WILL ACCEPT ME IN THE DOGBERT CULT.

YOU DO HAVE A STRONG RÉSUMÉ...

LOOKS LIKE YOU'VE BEEN FLEECED BY SEVERAL SPIRITUAL LEADERS ALREADY.

I THINK THAT DEMONSTRATES A COMPLETE ABSENCE OF INDEPENDENT THOUGHT.

CAN YOU CHANT?

I don't usually laugh at my own jokes, but the phrase, "Can you chant?" kills me every time I reread it.

TODAY ON "GERALDO" OUR ENTIRE SHOW IS ABOUT A DOG WHO STARTED HIS OWN CULT!

ACTUALLY, GERALDO, I DON'T KNOW WHAT YOU'RE TALKING ABOUT.

I LOVE LIVE TELEVISION.

This is why "Geraldo" is taped.

OUR TOP STORY: A DOG WITH GLASSES WAS SEEN BLOWING UP EMPTY MAIL TRUCKS WITH SOME TYPE OF "SONIC OBLITERATOR."

MUCH OF THE CITY IS IN RUINS, AS THE DOG BLASTED THROUGH BUILDINGS TO ESCAPE POLICE AND NATIONAL GUARD PURSUIT.

ON THE PLUS SIDE, WE HAVE A MUCH BETTER SHORTCUT TO THE POST OFFICE.

what happens when small weapons get more powerful? I hope I'm the first to get one on my block, while it's there.

THIS AUTHENTIC CHUNK OF THE BERLIN WALL IS THE LATEST ACQUISITION OF MY MUSEUM.

HEY! YOU MUST THINK WE'RE A COUPLE OF HILLBILLIES. WE SAW A HOLE IN YOUR SIDEWALK IN THAT EXACT SHAPE.

OBVIOUSLY WE HAD TO TRADE A CHUNK OF OUR SIDEWALK TO BERLIN SO WE COULD GET THIS.

APOLOGIZE TO THE DOG, FLOSSIE.

I have a chunk of the Berlin wall. I mean, I think I have one.

WHEN I CONQUER THE EARTH... WILL IT BE MORE EFFICIENT TO PUT ALL HUMANS IN PRISON...

...OR TRAIN THEM AS DOMESTIC SERVANTS FOR DOGS?

IT'S AMAZING HOW DOGS CAN SIT FOR HOURS THINKING ABSOLUTELY NOTHING.

what do you think they're thinking about?

DILBERT

By Scott Adams

WHY DO DOGS TWITCH THEIR FEET WHEN THEY SLEEP?

ZZZZ

IT'S SO CUTE. THEY MUST BE DREAMING ABOUT CHASING CARS.

HA HA! I AM SAINT DOGBERT! LINE UP TO KISS MY FEET, YOU KNAVES!

WHAT'S ON MY SCHEDULE TODAY, LACKEY?

YOU'LL BE PUSHING WHINEY, UGLY PEOPLE INTO MUD AT NINE.

7-14

THEN, YOU'LL TEASE CATS ABOUT THEIR GROOMING METHODS UNTIL TEN.

GOOD, GOOD.

THEN YOU'LL RAISE TAXES, GO TO LUNCH, AND TAKE THE REST OF THE DAY OFF.

© 1991 United Feature Syndicate, Inc.

REALITY: WHAT A GYP.

J. Adams

This is what I dream about too.

118

I AM DOGBERT, THE SUPREME RULER OF EARTH!!

WORSHIP ME, YOU IGNORANT MASSES!!

THAT WAS PRACTICE.

DARN, NOW MY EYES ARE STUCK IN ZOMBIE MODE...

© 1991 United Feature Syndicate, Inc.

9-23

I'll bet some readers went into spontaneous zombie mode when they read this.

HEY! YOU CHARGED ME TEN DOLLARS YESTERDAY!

PET ME $5⁰⁰

FIVE DOLLARS IS JUST THE BASE PRICE. I CHARGE EXTRA FOR AN EXTENDED NO-RABIES WARRANTY AND OTHER ADD-ONS.

10-29

I'LL TAKE A "PLAIN."

WAG OR NO WAG?

© 1991 United Feature Syndicate, Inc.

Who makes the rules about who can touch other creatures and how? It all seems kinda arbitrary to me.

I'VE DECIDED TO RUN FOR PRESIDENT OF THE UNITED STATES.

I'M HOPING MY CHARISMA WILL UNIFY A DIVIDED POLITICAL PARTY.

2-24

YOU'RE RUNNING AS A DEMOCRAT?

NO, COMMUNIST. I WANT TO HAVE A CHANCE.

© 1992 United Feature Syndicate, Inc.

This joke made sense in 1992. Trust me.

119

WHAT'S THIS?

I'M STARTING MY OWN NEWSLETTER FOR CLUELESS PEOPLE.

THANKS TO THE TECHNICAL MARVEL OF DESKTOP PUBLISHING, CLUELESS PEOPLE WILL NOW HAVE THE BENEFIT OF MY IMMENSE WISDOM.

HOW DO YOU KNOW WHO THE CLUELESS PEOPLE ARE?

THEY ASK A LOT OF QUESTIONS.

Shouldn't there be a newsletter for the clueless?

BOB, HERE'S A COPY OF MY NEW NEWSLETTER FOR CLUELESS PEOPLE.

"DOGBERT'S CLUES FOR THE CLUELESS:
1. PROFESSIONAL WRESTLING IS ALL FAKED.
2. NOBODY EVER LOST WEIGHT ON A HOME EXERCISE DEVICE."

" 3. LOOKS ARE MORE IMPORTANT TO HAPPINESS THAN BRAINS
4. IF PEOPLE DON'T COMMENT ON YOUR NEW HAIRDO, THEY HATE IT."

IT'S NOT HEALTHY TO READ THEM ALL AT ONCE, BOB.

IT'S A MIRACLE, RATBERT. THE IMAGE OF SAINT TED APPEARED IN MY JAR OF PEANUT BUTTER!

SAINT TED? WHO EVER HEARD OF SAINT TED? COULDN'T YOU GET SAINT THERESA?

SHE WAS BOOKED TO A CAN OF VARNISH IN UPSTATE NEW YORK.

SAINT TED LOOKS LIKE A "HAPPY FACE."

If there's a Hell, I'm going there for sure.

"ALTHOUGH RAISING CHILDREN IS DIFFICULT, BE ASSURED THAT YOU WILL GET HELP FROM A POWER GREATER THAN YOURSELF."

"TEACH YOUR CHILDREN ABOUT THE HIGHER POWER AND ABOUT THE 'GREAT BOOK' WHICH WILL GIVE THEM DIRECTION."

THEY'RE CALLED "TV LISTINGS." WITHOUT THEM, YOU'RE JUST FLIPPING.

Is that the ugliest baby you ever saw?

LOOKS EASY ENOUGH.

HYPNOSIS FOR WORLD CONQUEST

HI, DOGBERT! WHAT ARE YOU READING?

NOTHING. YOU WILL REMEMBER NOTHING

WHO AM I? WHERE AM I?

THAT WAS A LITTLE BIT LIKE SAND-BLASTING A SOUP CRACKER.

If hypnosis worked, wouldn't all the leaders be hypnotists? What if they are?

THIS IS DOGBERT... YOU ARE ALL UNDER MY HYPNOTIC POWERS...

I AM THE SUPREME RULER OF EARTH. YOU MUST ALL CARRY DOGBERT POSTERS AND CHANT "DOGBERT IS MY KING."

THAT IS ALL FOR NOW. IF I THINK OF ANY-THING ELSE IMPORTANT I'LL LET YOU KNOW.

...IS MY KING

YOU HAVE TO ADMIT IT— SINCE DOGBERT CONQUERED THE EARTH WE'VE HAD NO WARS AND THE ECONOMY IMPROVED.

IT COULD BE A COINCIDENCE. ALL HE'S ORDERED SO FAR IS THAT WE CARRY HIS PICTURE AND WEAR BRASSIERES.

I THINK YOU'RE AFRAID OF CHANGE.

OH YEAH? WELL, I DON'T THINK YOU'RE A "D" CUP.

I favor the "Playful Despot" form of government.

WHAT ARE YOU MAKING?

COMMEMORATIVE COLLECTIBLE PLATES.

ONE OF THE MYSTERIES OF LIFE IS THAT YOU CAN PUT ANY PICTURE ON A PLATE AND HORDES OF MORONS WILL WANT TO OWN IT.

WOW! AN ACORN! AND IT'S ON A PLATE!

WHAT'S IT LIKE TO BE A MEMBER OF A HORDE?

If I ever understand why people collect plates, I will know everything there is to know about people.

IT LOOKS LIKE SALES OF THE "DOGBERT JOGGEROBIC CARPET PATCH" ARE BRISK.

YEAH, AND I'M LOOKING TO EXPAND.

RATBERT IS BUSY RESEARCHING NEW PRODUCT CONCEPTS FOR THE CARPET PATCH.

"CARPET CLUB FOR MEN."

I'd buy it.

I'M A LOUD DOG! GIVE ME A JOB! YOU MUST OBEY ME BECAUSE I'M LOUD!

OKAY OKAY

THAT WAS TOO EASY. THERE MUST BE SOMETHING WRONG WITH THE JOB. IT MUST BE AN ENTRY LEVEL JOB...

I WANT A RAISE!! PROMOTE ME, YOU IMBECILE!!

BAD TREND

10-4

Dogbert continues to get aggressive. Here he's channeling the personality of a loud co-worker from my cubicle days.

HA! MY TECHNIQUE OF BEING LOUD IS WORKING. I GOT A JOB AND A RAISE IN ONE DAY.

NOW I NEED AN OFFICE.

HEY! I WANT YOUR OFFICE NOW!!

WAIT... I MIGHT BE ABLE TO USE THE FRAME FOR SOMETHING!!

10-5

WOULD YOU LIKE TO SIGN THIS PETITION TO END WORLD HUNGER AT NO COST TO YOU?

END HUNGER

12-31

WORLD HUNGER? WHY DOES IT SAY "I DEMAND ELIMINATION OF THE GOVERNMENT AND THE ESTABLISHMENT OF A DOGBERT MONARCHY"?

IT'S STANDARD BOILERPLATE. THE LAWYERS INSISTED.

MAN, THOSE GUYS ARE IN A WORLD OF THEIR OWN.

END

Have you ever insisted on carefully reading a petition before signing? It makes the **123** gatherers nervous.

This concept is based on an ex-co-worker's philosophy. It worked quite well.

Here's a story line that wasn't as fun on paper as it was in my head...

...But I was working my day job and couldn't afford to throw the cartoon out and 124→ do another. So I confessed.

. . . Saving Dilbert

DILBERT HIRES A CLEANING PERSON

AND YOUR NAME IS ..?

CALL ME MR. TIDY.

THE AGENCY SAYS YOU'RE EXPERIENCED.

YEAH, I'VE CLEANED OUT SOME OF THE NICER HOMES IN THIS AREA

THE BEST THING HERE IS TO LOAD YOUR POSSESSIONS INTO MY VAN, AND I'LL CLEAN 'EM AT MY PLACE.

WILL THAT COST ME EXTRA?

I try to make the criminals non-stereotypical and caucasian so I don't get beat up.

DOGBERT, WHERE'S ALL OF OUR FURNITURE?!!

YOUR NEW CLEANING PERSON LOADED IT INTO HIS VAN AND DROVE AWAY... OH, AND HE SAID TO TELL YOU HE QUIT.

I THINK WE NEED TO REVIEW YOUR JOB DESCRIPTION AS WATCH DOG.

I GOT HIS ADDRESS.

SEND MY check to 1348 OKE WALNUT TO

Dogbert only <u>seems</u> non-dangerous.

DILBERT THE VIGILANTE

WHEN I GET HOME FROM WORK, WE'LL TRACK DOWN THE MAN WHO ROBBED OUR HOUSE AND MAKE HIM PAY!!

NO! IT'S THE ROBBER AT MY DESK. HE'S STEALING MY JOB TOO!

HE'S AN IMPOSTER. LOOK AT HIS HAIR!

WE THOUGHT YOU'D BEEN IN A STREET FIGHT WITH VIDAL SASSOON.

A reader told me that Vidal Sassoon was actually a tough character in his —**125**→ wilder youth. I don't know if it's true.

This was my version of a touching "Lassie" plot.

Ultimately, Dogbert will always rescue Dilbert.

Remember, stalagmites might hang from the ceiling, but they don't.

126

DILBERT'S EXPENSE VOUCHER

WHAT ARE YOU TRYING TO PULL?? DO YOU THINK WE'RE IDIOTS IN ACCOUNTING?!!

NO, I SWEAR, I THINK YOU'RE SMART BUT SADISTIC TROLLS WITH MANY HUMANOID CHARACTERISTICS.

APPARENTLY THERE WAS NO RIGHT ANSWER.

I have to turn the paper upside down to draw Dilbert upside down.

DILBERT'S EXPENSE VOUCHER

YOU SPENT NEARLY $10 PER DAY ON MEALS DURING YOUR TRIP.

THE TRAVEL GUIDELINES REQUIRE YOU TO STUN A PIGEON WITH YOUR BRIEFCASE ON THE WAY TO THE HOTEL THEN FRY IT UP ON YOUR TRAVEL IRON.

I TRIED...BUT IT WAS TAKING SO LONG.

TRY THE "WOOL" SETTING.

I love to write dialogue for two characters who are equally defective but in different ways.

DILBERT IS TRAPPED IN THE BOWELS OF ACCOUNTING

I UNDERSTAND YOU HAVE DILBERT IN THERE. FREE HIM, OR ELSE...

ELSE WHAT?

OR ELSE I WILL PUT THIS CAP ON MY HEAD BACKWARDS! YOUR LITTLE HARDWIRED ACCOUNTING BRAIN WILL EXPLODE JUST LOOKING AT IT.

WHAT WAS THAT POPPING SOUND?

A PARADIGM SHIFTING WITHOUT A CLUTCH.

I got lots of mail about this one. Many people didn't understand it. Others loved it.

HERE WE HAVE A LAB RAT, SPECIALLY BRED TO BE SUSCEPTIBLE TO PEER PRESSURE.

7-23

HOW ABOUT A BREWSKI?

I DON'T DRINK.

ALL THE COOL RATS DRINK BEER.

OKAY.

OF COURSE, THERE'S MORE TO SCIENCE THAN JUST HURTING ANIMALS, BUT FRANKLY IT'S THE PART I LIKE BEST.

This is the very first Ratbert appearance. I wasn't planning to make him a regular.

DOC, WE HAVE TO TALK.

EVERYDAY YOU FEED ME OVER A HUNDRED POUNDS OF MACARONI AND CHEESE ... AT FIRST I THOUGHT YOU WERE JUST BEING A GOOD HOST.

BUT LATELY I'VE BEEN THINKING IT COULD BE SOMETHING FAR MORE SINISTER.

MACARONI AND CHEESE CAUSES PARANOIA...

7-24

This is based loosely on the old "frogs with no legs are deaf" joke.

WHAT'S THAT NOISE?

SKRITCH SKRITCH SKRITCH

7-26

IT SOUNDS LIKE A RAT, ESCAPED FROM A NEARBY LABORATORY, CHEWING A HOLE THROUGH OUR FRONT DOOR TO AVOID SURE DEATH FROM A HIDEOUS MACARONI-AND-CHEESE EXPERIMENT.

THAT'S AMAZING.

THESE BABIES AREN'T JUST FOR GOOD LOOKS, YOU KNOW.

Sometimes it's hard to review the plot so you can get to the next joke. **128**

Ratbert was an unplanned addition to the **Dilbert** cast. It all started with one series of jokes about a gullible lab rat who thought he was being fed massive amounts of food simply because the scientist was a polite host.

Ratbert's scientist could only afford one rat because of budget cutbacks. That meant that he had to keep Ratbert alive from one experiment to the next. (It also meant I didn't have to draw a lot of rat "extras" standing around in the scene.)

I like to keep my characters on the edge of awareness about their situation. In this case Ratbert was starting to get suspicious about the motives of the scientist. His innocence and exuberance were personally amusing to me and easy to write. The challenge was integrating him with Dilbert's household.

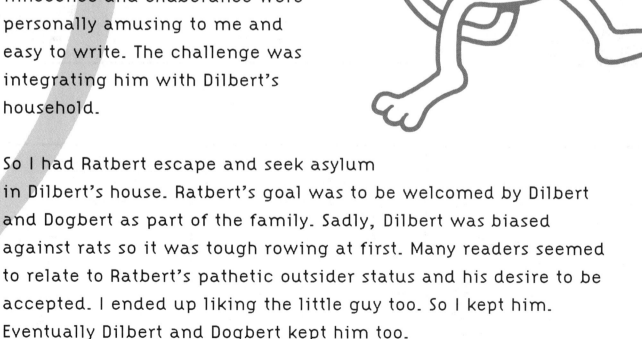

So I had Ratbert escape and seek asylum in Dilbert's house. Ratbert's goal was to be welcomed by Dilbert and Dogbert as part of the family. Sadly, Dilbert was biased against rats so it was tough rowing at first. Many readers seemed to relate to Ratbert's pathetic outsider status and his desire to be accepted. I ended up liking the little guy too. So I kept him. Eventually Dilbert and Dogbert kept him too.

GREETINGS, DOG. I'VE COME TO LIVE IN YOUR HOUSE AND ESCAPE FROM MY JOB AT THE LABORATORY.

YOU COULD THINK OF ME AS A POLITICAL EXILE SEEKING SANCTUARY IN A FRIENDLY EMBASSY.

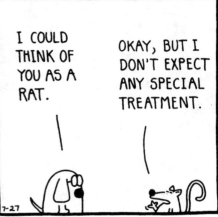

I COULD THINK OF YOU AS A RAT.

OKAY, BUT I DON'T EXPECT ANY SPECIAL TREATMENT.

At first, Ratbert can't imagine why anyone would be prejudiced against rats.

I WASN'T GETTING ANY RESPECT AT THE LAB . . . I FELT USED.

SURE . . . THE FOOD WAS GOOD — AND LOTS OF IT . . . BUT I DON'T THINK THE PROFESSOR VALUED ME AS AN INDIVIDUAL.

AND A RAT WITHOUT RESPECT IS LIKE . . . LIKE . . .

LIKE YOU.

I often felt like Ratbert in my cubicle maze.

DILBERT, THIS IS A RAT. RAT, THIS IS DILBERT.

I'VE COME TO LIVE HERE!

HOW LUCKY FOR US. WE WERE JUST SAYING HOW MUCH WE NEEDED A PLAGUE-CARRYING VERMIN TO ROUND OUT THE HOUSEHOLD.

HE DOESN'T HAVE MUCH OF A PERSONALITY...

I USUALLY DROWN HIM OUT WITH THE TELEVISION.

Dilbert is particularly closed-minded about rats.

Panel 1: IF YOU'RE GOING TO LIVE HERE, YOU NEED A NAME. / HOW ABOUT "MICKEY"?

Panel 2: NO... BIG TROUBLE. HOW ABOUT "RODNEY THE RODENT"? / HOW ABOUT "BILL THE RAT"?

7-31

Panel 3: "VERNON THE VERMIN"? / "RATBERT"

Ratbert was the first "bert" after Dogbert, thus establishing a pattern.

Panel 4: LET ME INTRODUCE YOU TO OUR DINOSAURS, BOB AND DAWN. / COOL!

8-1

Panel 5: EEEEK!! A MOUSE! / NOT A MOUSE, A RAT!!

Panel 6: OOPS. SORRY. YOU LOOK KINDA LIKE A MOUSE. / NO OFFENSE TAKEN.

Ratbert is prejudiced against mice.

Panel 7: AHAA! THERE'S MY RUNAWAY LAB RAT! I'D RECOGNIZE LITTLE XP-39C^2 ANYWHERE!

Panel 8: ALL IS FORGIVEN. COME BACK TO YOUR JOB AT THE LAB. I LOVE YOU.

Panel 9: HE WAS SPECIALLY BRED TO HAVE NO WILL POWER. / HOLD ME.

8-3

Here's a good trivia question: what was Ratbert's original name?

131

A SCIENTIST REPORTS THAT LOVE MADE A LAB RAT STUPID.

THE SCIENTIST CAUTIONED THE MEDIA NOT TO DRAW CONCLUSIONS BASED ON ONE RAT.

© 1990 United Feature Syndicate, Inc.

TIME

LOVE AND S.A.T. SCORES

If it weren't for lack of context, there would be no news.

THERE'S A TERRIBLE STIGMA TO BEING A RAT . . .

I ONCE PAINTED A POUCH ON MY STOMACH AND TOLD PEOPLE I WAS A TINY KANGA-ROO

THAT'S WHEN I FOUND OUT THAT PEOPLE HATE TINY KANGAROOS.

© 1991 United Feature Syndicate, Inc.

Don't you love the phrase "Tiny kangaroos"?

ALL THIS WEEK I'VE BEEN TESTING MADONNA'S "COMPULSION" PERFUME AT THE LAB.

ANY SIDE EFFECTS?

HECK NO . . . UNLESS YOU CONSIDER MARRYING A BUNSEN BURNER A "SIDE EFFECT."

SAY . . . WHO'S THAT CUTE LITTLE FILLY ON THE TABLE ?!

WE CALL HER THE LAMP.

© 1991 United Feature Syndicate, Inc.

what if perfume actually did what it promised?

WHAT DO YOU THINK OF MY CHIHUAHUA DISGUISE?!

IT'S A GOOD START, RATBERT, BUT IT TAKES MORE THAN A TURTLENECK TO LOOK LIKE A CHIHUAHUA.

HOW ABOUT IF I MAKE THIS FACE AND ACT NERVOUS?

PERFECT.

↶ words to live by.

WHY DOES DOGBERT ALWAYS GET TO SIT ON YOUR LEGS AND I NEVER DO?

BECAUSE DOGBERT IS MY BEST FRIEND AND YOU'RE JUST A DISEASE-CARRYING VERMIN.

MAYBE THIS ISN'T THE TIME TO LAUNCH MY "FAMILY HUG TIME" CONCEPT.

Ratbert begins the full-court press for family acceptance.

FORGET DOGBERT; I CAN BE YOUR NEW BEST FRIEND!

RATS ARE TWICE AS GOOD FOR CUDDLING. AND YOU SHOULD SEE ME CATCH A FRISBEE!

HERE, SCRATCH BEHIND MY EARS. YOU'LL FIND ME MOST APPRECIATIVE!

YOU SOUND LIKE ME ON A DATE.

I'VE DEVELOPED A PLAN TO MAKE YOU PITY ME AND THEN WELCOME ME IN YOUR FAMILY.

I BUILT TIMMY THE TOILET PAPER MAN. TIMMY WILL BE MY ONLY FRIEND. IT WILL BE SO PATHETIC AND HEART-RENDING THAT YOU WILL HAVE TO LOVE ME.

DILBERT SEEMS TO HAVE VERY LITTLE RESPECT FOR TIMMY.

I'm surprised I got away with this one.

I'M TESTING A GROWTH FORMULA AT THE LAB.

I'M SO HAPPY. I'VE OFTEN THOUGHT THAT THE ONLY THING BETTER THAN A RAT IN THE HOUSE IS A GIANT RAT IN THE HOUSE.

YESTERDAY I WOULD HAVE BEEN MIFFED AT YOUR SARCASM. BUT THAT WOULDN'T BE "BIG" OF ME.

BETTER YET, A GIANT, WITTY RAT.

Ratbert got bigger because it was easier to draw him that way around the other characters.

THERE'S DILBERT... I'LL SNEAK UP AND HUG HIS LEG UNTIL HE LOVES ME AND ACCEPTS ME IN THE FAMILY.

A RAT IS CLINGING TO MY LEG.

I HAD THAT PROBLEM TILL I SWITCHED TO "OLD SPICE."

I WAS WONDERING IF WE'RE A DYSFUNCTIONAL FAMILY.

YOU'RE NOT A FAMILY MEMBER. YOU'RE A RAT WHO WON'T GO AWAY.

SUDDENLY I HAVE THE URGE TO ROB A CONVENIENCE STORE.

Ratbert is easy to write for because he's so cute. Anything he says sounds funnier because of that.

WHAT ARE THOSE DISHES DOING ON DILBERT'S HEAD?

HE'S IN A VIDEO GAME TRANCE. I'M TESTING MY THEORY THAT HE IS UNAWARE OF HIS ENVIRONMENT AND HAS NO DISCERNABLE MENTAL ACTIVITY.

POOR GUY.

WHAT A TEAM WE MAKE, BOB!

NOW I WON'T NEED TO ACT PATHETIC TO GET LOVE. I'LL GET ALL THE SPILLOVER LOVE THAT PEOPLE NATURALLY HAVE FOR DINOSAURS!

EWW! IT'S A HUGE LIZARD WITH A TALKING ZIT. I'M GONNA BE SICK.

GREAT... I GOT A DEFECTIVE DINOSAUR.

Paired with Bob the Dinosaur, there's almost too much cuteness.

135

Things are looking bad for Ratbert...

Finally, Ratbert is accepted in the family.

Like any family member, Ratbert is free to be annoying.

SINCE YOU WON'T GO AWAY, I'LL MAKE YOU AN INTERN.

GREAT! WHAT'S AN INTERN?

YOU'LL SPEND YOUR DAY IN A HIGH-TRAFFIC CUBE TRYING TO LOOK BUSY. YOUR MAIN FUNCTION IS TO MAKE THE REST OF US GLAD WE'RE NOT YOU.

HOW DID PEOPLE EVER LOOK BUSY BEFORE COMPUTERS?

Ratbert is perfect for low-ego jobs.

I'M GOING TO INTERVIEW SUCCESSFUL PEOPLE AND WRITE A BOOK OF THEIR TIPS. I'LL START WITH YOU, DOGBERT.

SET YOUR ALARM CLOCK TO GO OFF EVERY HOUR. KEEP A BIG VAT OF "JELL-O" BY THE BED. WHEN THE ALARM GOES OFF, STICK YOUR HEAD IN THE "JELL-O" AND YELL "BOY, I'M TIRED!"

THANKS!

BEWARE THE ADVICE OF SUCCESSFUL PEOPLE; THEY DO NOT SEEK COMPANY.

Do you think successful people tell <u>all</u> of their secrets?

MY INSPIRATIONAL POSTERS AREN'T WORKING. I NEED TO DO SOME ANIMAL RESEARCH, RATBERT.

READY!!

IN THIS BEAUTIFUL SCENE WE SEE A MIGHTY EAGLE SWOOPING DOWN TO CAPTURE ITS PREY. WHAT IS YOUR REACTION?

I THINK IT'S WORKING.

RUN FOR IT, MOM!!!

Has anyone <u>ever</u> been inspired by a poster?

I like the idea of geniuses existing around us in unlikely professions.

If a genius does something that doesn't make sense to me, why do I think he's wrong?

GARBAGEMAN

Dilbert's **Garbageman** is the world's smartest human. I like putting incongruous things together. The unanswered question about this character is why he would choose to be a garbageman if he was the smartest man in the world. But if you think about it, we wouldn't be in a position to judge anything done by the world's smartest person. Obviously his decisions would be different from our own—he's smarter! So if we don't understand why he does what he does, the problem is probably on our end.

MAYBE I'LL NEVER SOLVE THE MYSTERY OF WHY DILBERT'S NECKTIES CURL UP.

SOMETIMES, DOGBERT, LIFE PRESENTS US WITH MYSTERIES TO FUEL OUR SENSE OF WONDER... IT STIMULATES US TO REACH BEYOND OURSELVES TO SOMETHING GREATER.

THIS ISN'T ONE OF THOSE TIMES, IS IT?

APPARENTLY NOT.

WHAT HAPPENED WITH THE ROBOT YOU WERE BUILDING?

NOBODY CAN MAKE A ROBOT. IT'S IMPOSSIBLE.

HMM... A PERFECTLY GOOD ROBOT. PROBABLY JUST NEEDS A NEURO-SPECTRUM FIELD CALIBRATION.

THAT WHOLE ROBOT PROJECT WAS BAD FOR MY EGO AS AN ENGINEER.

HEY! GUESS WHO'S WAY SMARTER THAN YOU!

I knew a garbage man who found great stuff in the trash and fixed it up. He was literally smarter than his customers in almost every way. I admired him.

FROM THE LOOKS OF YOUR GARBAGE, YOU'VE INVENTED SOME SORT OF MOLECULE BIFURCATION COMMUNICATOR.

AH, YES, EINSTEIN THOUGHT THIS TYPE OF THING MIGHT WORK. PHYSICIST JOHN STUART BELL KIND OF FLESHED IT OUT IN 1964. BUT YOU'VE REALLY ADDED SOMETHING...

SPECIFICALLY, YOU'VE ADDED THIS CALCULATION ERROR HERE.

I WISH YOU'D REALIZE THAT YOU'RE A GARBAGE MAN, NOT AN ENGINEER. I DON'T NEED YOUR SUGGESTIONS ON MY DESIGNS.

WHAT ARE YOU WRITING? OH YEAH, AS IF I CARE.

IF YOU NEED HELP UNDERSTANDING THAT, THE PAPER BOY WILL BE BY SOON. I'VE BEEN WORKING WITH HIM.

I get many suggestions from non-cartoonists. The worst part is that many of them are good.

DILBERT WON'T BUILD A PHASER PISTOL FOR ME. HE THINKS IT'S WRONG TO ZAP PEOPLE FOR FUN.

YEAH, THAT WOULD BE WRONG... UNLESS THE PEOPLE YOU ZAP ARE THEMSELVES IMMORAL, IN WHICH CASE YOU WOULD BE ON THE SIDE OF JUSTICE.

I GUESS IT'S ACADEMIC SINCE I DON'T HAVE A PHASER.

HERE, BORROW MINE.

I wish I had a phaser.

DILBERT, YOU'LL BE PLAYING THE LEFT STRIKER POSITION.

ONE OF OUR GOOD PLAYERS WILL TRY TO STRIKE YOU IN THE HEAD WITH THE BALL AND BANK IT IN THE GOAL.

"IT" BEING THE BALL, NOT YOUR HEAD.

I'D BETTER TAKE OFF MY GLASSES.

NO, DON'T. I INCLUDED THEIR DAMPENING EFFECT IN MY CALCULATIONS.

6-16

I played in a co-ed soccer league. We lost every game. I kept watching my teammates instead of the ball.

BONK

GEE, I'VE SCORED FIVE GOALS THAT WAY

YOU'VE GOT A GOOD HEAD FOR THIS GAME.

6-17

I wanted Liz to look athletic, but she looks 12 years old.

LIZ, I NOTICED YOU'RE NOT WEARING A RING. WOULD YOU LIKE TO GO FOR A PIZZA AFTER THE GAME?

OH, I DO HAVE A RING. IT'S SO BIG I CAN'T WEAR IT. A TEAM OF EUNUCHS FOLLOWS ME AROUND WITH IT IN A SPECIAL VAN.

6-18

FLOP-SWEAT TIME.

YOU'RE GULLIBLE. I LIKE THAT.

Hey, It's hard to draw soccer balls! You try it.

LIZ

I created **Liz** so Dilbert could experience having a girlfriend. Liz is a materials engineer and a good soccer player. She likes brainy guys and she has very big hair. That's all we know about her.

Many readers asked me to allow Dilbert to lose his innocence with Liz, so to speak. But I didn't see any way I could do that in a comic strip and get it past the editors. So I developed a secret sign. I told the people who receive the **Dilbert** newsletter that if Dilbert ever got lucky with Liz, I would draw his normally upturned necktie flat one day. I expected a flood of e-mail from people encouraging me to do it.

I was wrong.

The women who wrote were almost unanimous in their desire for Dilbert to get lucky. But the men were split evenly. Half wanted Dilbert to do the deed and half said, in effect, "I don't think Dilbert should get lucky until I do."

Apparently a large segment of the male population was using Dilbert as a yardstick of their own success with women and they didn't want to fall any further behind.

Now I had a problem.

I ended up finessing the situation by writing a strip with an intentionally ambiguous ending. Everyone had the option of thinking his view prevailed. Here is the lead up to the flat tie strip.

My biggest problem with Liz is that I'm not very good at drawing attractive female characters. People told me she looked twelve years old. And she never really clicked with me or the readers, so I eventually gave up on her and had her break up with Dilbert. I don't know if she'll be back.

I'M A NINETIES KIND OF WOMAN. I DEMAND EQUALITY BUT THE MAN MUST PAY FOR DINNER.

AND RECENT SURVEYS SHOW THAT MANY WOMEN MY AGE THINK IT'S OKAY TO SLAP A MAN.

REALLY? DID THEY NAME THE MAN?

DON'T MAKE ME COME OVER THERE.

I CAN TELL THAT YOU LIKE ME BECAUSE YOU DON'T QUITE KNOW WHAT TO DO WITH YOUR HANDS.

TO TEST MY HYPOTHESIS I WILL HOLD THIS HAND AND OBSERVE THE CHANGE.

THE "CONTROL" HAND REMAINS LIMP AND CLAMMY. ITS TWIN LOSES CONTROL. HYPOTHESIS CONFIRMED.

THUPA THUPA THUPA THUPA THUPA

I liked the concept of Liz being a science wonk.

I THINK I FOUND A WOMAN WHO LIKES ME, DOGBERT.

NO WAY!

IT'S PHIL, THE PRINCE OF INSUFFICIENT LIGHT!

HECK JUST FROZE OVER.

THIS IS NOT MY FAULT!

TELL THEM.

THIS WAS OUR THIRD DATE, LIZ. TRADITION DEMANDS THAT YOU KISS ME OR GIVE ME THE "LET'S BE FRIENDS" TALK.

7-2

NO, OUR FIRST DATE ONLY COUNTED AS 85% OF A DATE BECAUSE WE WERE WEARING OUR SWEAT PANTS.

I'M 15% SHORT?!!

IT'S TOO BAD, BECAUSE I REALLY FELT LIKE KISSING.

Everyone understands the third date rule, right?

IT SEEMS ALMOST UNNATURAL FOR ME TO HAVE AN ACTUAL GIRLFRIEND.

WHY?

IT'S LIKE WHEN THE CAPTAIN ON "STAR TREK" FALLS IN LOVE, AND YOU KNOW THE WOMAN WILL DIE IN AN UNLIKELY ACCIDENT.

HEY! WE JUST SAW OUR FIRST SHOOTING STAR!

7-25

I was toying with the idea of bumping Liz off, but this was as close as it got.

LIZ, IF YOU'RE GOING TO CONTINUE SEEING DILBERT, YOU'LL HAVE TO PASS MY TEST.

QUESTION ONE: GIVE SEVEN HUNDRED REASONS WHY DOGS ARE SUPERIOR TO CATS.

11-25

WELL, THE FIRST SIX HUNDRED REASONS HAVE TO DO WITH THE FACT THAT YOU'RE CUTER.

FINGERNAILS! SHE-DEVIL!

Liz would have to be acceptable to Dogbert.

Liz had to like Dilbert's nerdiness or the relationship made no sense.

I suspect this scene has happened a million times in real life.

I have the cutest little laptop. I love that thing.

what about me? I drew a cartoon about reading a book about a simulation...

Why is the floor more comfortable than the couch?

IN THE YEAR THAT WE'VE DATED, LIZ, YOU'VE OFTEN MENTIONED VARIOUS PROBLEMS IN YOUR LIFE.

I HAVE COMPILED THOSE PROBLEMS INTO A LIST OF REQUIREMENTS AND DEVELOPED A COMPREHENSIVE SET OF SOLUTIONS.

HOW THOUGHTFUL. I DIDN'T EVEN KNOW I WAS BROKEN.

NO, NO, NOT BROKEN... JUST A BIT BUGGY.

The end is near.

I'VE DECIDED TO DATE OTHER MEN.

NOOO!!! DON'T BREAK UP WITH ME!

I'M NOT. I JUST WANT TO DATE OTHER MEN AT THE SAME TIME.

I AM **NOT** HAPPY RIGHT NOW.

THAT'S EXACTLY WHY I NEED A SPARE.

I know a woman who threatened her boy-friend by saying she would get an "additional" boyfriend.

LIZ STARTED DATING OTHER MEN. TWO CAN PLAY AT THAT GAME.

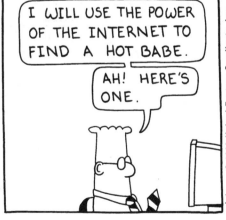

I WILL USE THE POWER OF THE INTERNET TO FIND A HOT BABE.

AH! HERE'S ONE.

SHE WANTS YOUR CREDIT CARD NUMBER.

OOH! SHE'S INQUISITIVE. I LIKE THAT.

People wrote to 150 warn me that chocolate is dangerous for dogs.

MOM & DAD

Mom and Dad Dilbert's mother—"The Dilmom," as some readers call her—is one of my favorite characters. She gives us an idea where Dilbert got his skill with technology. On the outside she's a cookie-baking, fifties sort of woman. But she reveals in small glimpses an incredible depth of technical skill and understanding.

Dilbert's father has never been seen in the strip, only referred to. He has been at the all-you-can-eat restaurant in the local mall for years. He won't leave until it's "all he can eat." The restaurant is open 24 hours a day so it has been a standoff so far. Dilbert gets his brains from his mother's side and his literalness from his dad. Put them together and you have a perfect engineer.

GOOD NEWS: THE "ALL-YOU-CAN-EAT" SALAD BAR JOINT JUST DECIDED TO STAY OPEN TWENTY-FOUR HOURS A DAY!

WE CAN GET A TABLE BY THE WINDOW AND LIVE THERE FOR THE REST OF OUR LIVES — FOR ONLY $5.95 APIECE!

1-5-90

S.Adams

HOW WOULD WE BATHE?

THEY HAVE LITTLE "MOIST TOWLETTES."

You just need lots of them.

IT'S REALLY DIFFERENT AROUND HERE SINCE WE LOST DILBERT'S DAD.

WHEN DID HE DIE?

HE'S NOT DEAD. WE LOST HIM AT THE MALL, CHRISTMAS OF '92.

S.Adams

SHOULDN'T YOU BE LOOKING FOR HIM?

I SAID IT'S DIFFERENT, NOT WORSE.

That's her hair, not a weird hat.

Panel 1: I CAN'T BELIEVE YOUR FATHER HAS BEEN LOST AT THE MALL SINCE 1992!

Panel 2: IF MY FATHER OR MY HUSBAND WERE LOST AT THE MALL I'D BE SEARCHING FOR HIM TWENTY-FOUR HOURS A DAY!!

Panel 3: WE'RE WAITING FOR A SALE.

YOU'RE A BIT OF A WHINER, AREN'T YOU, DEAR?

You can't tell if they're pulling Liz's leg. Even I don't know.

Panel 4: MY COMPANY ASKED ALL EMPLOYEES TO ACT AS SALESPEOPLE TO FRIENDS AND FAMILY. I THINK YOU COULD USE THIS, MOM.

Panel 5: WHY WOULD I NEED A PRIMARY RATE CIRCUIT? I'VE ALREADY GOT A FRAME RELAY DROP TO MY WEB SERVER IN THE SEWING ROOM.

Panel 6: THIS IS GOING TO BE A TOUGH SALE.

HELLO-O-O! EARTH TO DILBERT! THIS IS PACKET DATA...

I try to make sure the reader doesn't need to know the technology to get the point. But it's funnier if you realize Dilmom has a good point.

MY COMPUTER SIMULATION WILL DETERMINE, ONCE AND FOR ALL, THE REAL REASON DINOSAURS BECAME EXTINCT.

7-17

WAIT... ACCORDING TO THIS, IT WOULD BE ALMOST IMPOSSIBLE FOR ALL DINOSAURS TO BE EXTINCT.

THEN THEY MUST JUST BE...

S.Adams

© 1989 United Feature Syndicate, Inc.

...HIDING.

YEAH? JUST TRY TO FIND US.

SHHHH!

The strip wasn't doing too well in 1989, so I was looking for a hook to draw people in.

HEY... YOU WERE RIGHT. DINOSAURS AREN'T EXTINCT.

I'M BOB. SHE'S DAWN. WE WERE HIDING IN YOUR HOUSE.

© 1989 United Feature Syndicate, Inc.

7-19 S.Adams

ONLY ONE KIND OF DINOSAUR COULD HIDE THAT WELL...

CORRECT: A NOBODYSAURUS.

Everyone loves dinosaurs, right?

...SO DAWN HERE IS A NOBODYSAURUS, AND BOB, YOU SAY YOU'RE A THESAURUS?

HA HA! NO, THE "THESAURUS" LINE IS JUST AN OLD DINOSAUR JOKE.

HEE HEE!

7-20

© 1989 United Feature Syndicate, Inc.

I'LL BET YOU WERE A RIOT IN THE MESOZOIC ERA.

EAT HIM, BOB.

S.Adams

154

Dawn is the name of a friend of mine who has non-human thoughts on a regular basis.

Bob, Dawn, and Rex the Dinosaurs

Bob, Dawn, and Rex the Dinosaurs emerged after Dilbert calculated it was impossible for all dinosaurs to be extinct—therefore they must be hiding. And they were, in people's houses. Dinosaurs turned out to be smaller than we thought and able to hide very effectively.

Bob and Dawn were the two dinosaurs living in Dilbert's house. Later they gave birth to little Rex. Bob is dumb and easily excited. His favorite activity is giving wedgies to people who deserve it. His character is more fun than Dawn or Rex, so you won't see much of Bob's family. They continue to hide.

OKAY THEN, IF YOU TWO DINOSAURS WANT TO CONTINUE HIDING IN MY HOUSE YOU HAVE TO OBSERVE THE HOUSE RULES.

LET'S SEE ... UH ... REMAIN OUT OF SIGHT ... DON'T LEAVE THE LIGHTS ON WHEN YOU'RE OUT OF THE ROOM ...

S. Adams

AM I FORGETTING ANYTHING, DOGBERT?

HOW ABOUT "NO RIPPING THE FLESH OFF THE OTHER RESI- DENTS."

A rare action sequence.

I used to have that problem.

CAN WE TALK?

DAWN AND I WANT TO HAVE AN EGG.

AND YOU WANT MY BLESSING?

WE WANT INSTRUCTIONS.

MY "NATIONAL GEOGRAPHICS" STOP JUST SHORT...

If nobody taught humans how to mate, could they figure it out on their own?

WE WANT TO HAVE AN EGG, BUT WE DON'T KNOW HOW.

JUST DO WHAT COMES NATURALLY.

YOU MEAN... ROLL IN JELLO WHILE YODELING?

YOU'RE DOOMED.

HELLO, IS THIS THE LIBRARY REFERENCE DESK?

I HAVE THIS... ER... FRIEND... WHO WAS WONDERING HOW DINOSAURS HAVE EGGS.

UH-HUH...

IT'S GROSS.

The reference desk librarian knows everything!

Dinosaurs invite dumb jokes. It's not my fault.

I'm glad I wasn't born in an egg. It looks uncomfortable.

Rex is the name I would give myself if that were a graceful option.

Yikes! I just realized today is Father's Day and I haven't called home yet! (Really.)

I stopped listening to adults when I was about ten. I still don't.

159

TAKE BOB WITH YOU, NORIKO. YOU'LL NEED HELP SAVING THE PLANET FOR YOUR GENERATION.

6-5

I HAVE A BLACK BELT IN KARATE. WHAT SKILLS DO YOU BRING TO THE PARTY?

WEDGIES, MOSTLY.

S. Adams

IT'S NOT AS MENACING AS KARATE, BUT YOU HAVE TO LOVE THE EXPRESSIONS ON THEIR FACES.

TURN HIM THIS WAY.

© 1993 United Feature Syndicate, Inc.

Maybe Bob is a "Wedgie-sore-ass."

REMEMBER, BOB, IT IS BETTER TO GIVE TO DOGBERT THAN TO RECEIVE... ESPECIALLY AT CHRISTMAS

S. Adams

BUT I DON'T HAVE ANY INCOME... EXCEPT FOR THE COINS PEOPLE DROP WHEN I GIVE THEM WEDGIES.

12-22

© 1993 United Feature Syndicate, Inc.

IT SEEMS LIKE EXACTLY THE WRONG SEASON TO PICK UP THE PACE ON THIS SORT OF THING.

The tongue really ↗ sells this one.

FROM NOW ON, BOB PLEASE REFER TO ME AS A "RATTUS," NOT BY THE DIMINUTIVE TERM "RAT."

S. Adams

FRANKLY, I'VE NEVER THOUGHT OF FOLKS LIKE YOU IN TERMS OF YOUR GENUS. I SEE YOU AS PART OF A LARGER COMMUNITY.

REALLY?

© 1994 United Feature Syndicate, Inc.

YEAH — THE COMMUNITY OF THINGS THAT GO "SQEAK" WHEN I STEP ON THEM.

THAT'S SO FUNNY I FORGOT TO LAUGH.

5-27

161

RATBERT THE OPTIMIST

I FEEL LUCKY TODAY.

LUCKY, LUCKY, LUCKY.

I THINK A HAT JUST BLEW ONTO MY HEAD!!

This is the first appearance of Catbert.

BOB, I'LL YANK THE CAT OFF OF RATBERT'S HEAD AND YOU STOMP ON IT!

YANK
STOMP

I COULD HAVE PHRASED THAT BETTER.

I'M NOT AN OPTIMIST ANYMORE.

YOU'RE NOT WELCOME HERE, CAT. IT'S AGAINST HOUSE RULES TO EAT RATBERT.

MY WORK HERE IS NOT DONE UNTIL I HAVE POUNCED ON MY NATURAL ENEMY.

WHO ARE YOU, AND WHAT ARE YOU DOING ON MY KEYBOARD?

Cat owners understand that cats love to get on keyboards. Other people 162 were confused by this one.

CATBERT

Catbert was introduced for one series of strips involving an attack on Ratbert. I had no plans to keep the cat character. When readers saw him they wrote hundreds of e-mail messages requesting "more Catbert." The funny thing was, I had not named this character, yet everyone referred to him as Catbert. It seems to me that when hundreds of readers spontaneously and unanimously name a character for you, it's a good idea to keep him.

The challenge was figuring out how to integrate Catbert into the **Dilbert** world. I didn't want him to live under Dogbert's roof, and most of the action was happening in Dilbert's office. One day in the shower, inspiration came. I decided to make Catbert the Director of Human Resources at Dilbert's company. It's the perfect fit. Like H.R. directors, cats don't care if you live or die. And they enjoy playing with you before downsizing you.

GET OFF OF MY KEYBOARD, CAT, OR ELSE!

WATCH ME ACT LIKE I DON'T EVEN HEAR YOU.

CTRL-ALT-DEL

DOGBERT!

Catbert is fashioned after my fat gray cat, Freddie.

YOU HAVE TO GO, CAT. YOU HAVE NO VALUE TO US.

ACTUALLY, MY MERE EXISTENCE WILL WIDEN YOUR DEMO-GRAPHIC APPEAL AND MAKE YOU IMMORTAL.

OH... A CAT. THAT'S ORIGINAL.

GIVE IT A REST, "MICKEY."

PURR

I worried that adding a cat was not very original. But then I realized nothing else in the strip was original either, so I got over it.

I HIRED A NEW DIRECTOR OF HUMAN RESOURCES TO HANDLE THE DOWN-SIZING.

I NEEDED SOMEBODY WHO ACTS LIKE A FRIEND BUT SECRETLY DELIGHTS IN THE MISERY OF ALL PEOPLE.

WE NEED TO TALK, PAUL. BUT FIRST I'M GOING TO BAT YOUR HEAD AROUND AND SCRATCH YOU.

HEE HEE!! THAT'S SO CUTE!

Catbert has become a virtual mascot for Human Resources employees.

CATBERT THE HR DIRECTOR

HERE'S THE NEW ORG CHART. MAYBE YOU'RE ON IT AND MAYBE NOT.

OOH! NICE TRY! SO CLOSE. TOO BAD.

IT'S FUN TO PLAY WITH THEM BEFORE DOWNSIZING THEM.

Those aren't stripes on his back, just shading.

COME SEE THE NEW ORG CHART.

OOPS, CHANGED MY MIND!

WHAM!!

OUCHIE..

I'M SORE, BUT I'VE NEVER FELT SO FREE.

CATBERT THE HR DIRECTOR

I THINK I'LL INVENT SOME ILLOGICAL POLICIES TO ANNOY EMPLOYEES.

MY DIABOLICAL NEW DRESS CODE WILL MAKE THEM QUESTION THEIR OWN SANITY.

...SO, CASUAL CLOTHES DON'T LOWER OUR STOCK VALUE... BUT ONLY IF WORN ON FRIDAYS... UNLESS SOMEBODY SEES US... GOT IT?

I THINK I'M INSANE.

I know the concept of dress codes was invented by a cat.

who decided that jeans are not business clothes?
It seems like a random decision to me.

Many employees have been plagued by "dotted line"
bosses. I know I was.

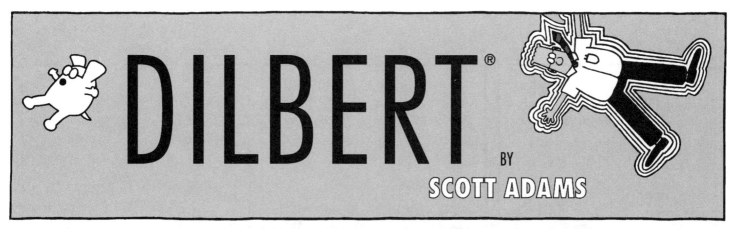

The "Total Compensation" concept is pulled from real life. It sounds much → **167** → better than "pay cut."

OH GOOD, THE LAST STOP OF THE DAY.

FREEZE, MORTAL! LET ME SEE THE EXPIRATION DATE ON THAT MILK!

I CAN GO TO HELL FOR DRINKING OLD MILK?!

NAH. I'M FROM "HECK." WE HANDLE THE LITTLE STUFF.

This is the first strip with Phil, The Prince of Insufficient light.

GOSH. I THOUGHT "HECK" WAS JUST A FIGURE OF SPEECH.

YEAH. A LOT OF PEOPLE THINK THEY CAN GET AWAY WITH MINOR INFRACTIONS.

ACCORDING TO MY RECORDS, LAST MONTH YOU DELIBERATELY ASKED FOR THREE LITTLE KETCHUPS AT McDONALD'S WHEN YOU KNEW YOU ONLY NEEDED TWO.

I KNEW THAT WOULD COME BACK TO HAUNT ME. LOOK, I STILL HAVE THE EXTRA ONE. I'LL GIVE IT BACK!

SHAME SHAME...

Can you tell he's holding a big spoon? It's not as scary as a pitchfork.

GEE, IF YOU'RE THE RULER OF "HECK" YOU MUST HAVE SOME KIND OF AWESOME NAME.

YEAH.

WELL, WHAT IS IT? SOMETHING LIKE "KING OF EVIL" OR "LORD OF DARKNESS"?

YOU CAN CALL ME PHIL, PRINCE OF INSUFFICIENT LIGHT.

168

Phil, The Prince of Insufficient Light

In my first year of syndication I tried to introduce Satan as a regular member of the **Dilbert** cast. My editor at United Media wisely advised against anything that would make me look like a Satan-worshiping cartoonist. (It doesn't take many complaints for a newspaper editor to decide to drop a new strip.) But I really wanted the devil character so I argued my case. After some negotiations, I ended up compromising and softening the character to its current form—Phil, Ruler of Heck, Prince of Insufficient Light. He wouldn't damn you, but he might darn you for minor infractions.

Oddly enough, the stripped-down, compromised version of Satan was much more interesting than the real thing would have been. So I'm quite pleased with the result. And to date I have not been accused of being in league with Phil, so it all worked out.

Many people who started reading **Dilbert** after Phil's introduction were confused by his occasional appearance. A number of people noted the facial similarity to the Pointy-Haired Boss and wondered if he was related. In truth, I just can't draw that many different faces, but I liked the suggestion that they might be brothers. And so it was revealed that in fact they are. I'm nothing if not flexible.

Sometimes Phil has a cape because I forget he isn't supposed to have one. **170**

LOOKS LIKE THEY UNDER-CHARGED ME TWELVE CENTS ON THE LETTUCE.

SHOP-WAY

© 1989 United Feature Syndicate, Inc.

10-3

I SHOULD GO BACK AND GIVE THEM THE TWELVE CENTS.

BUT I'M SURE THEY WOULD TELL ME TO KEEP IT FOR BEING SO HONEST.

S.Adams

...I HAVE A REPORT OF A FLIMSY RATIONALIZATION IN PROGRESS.

TRY THE KITCHEN.

S.Adams

HA! THE STORE UNDER-CHARGED ME TWELVE CENTS, AND I'M NOT TELLING THEM.

HEY!

10-4

I KNOW YOU. YOU'RE THE RULER OF HECK, THE "PRINCE OF INSUFFICIENT LIGHT."

JUST CALL ME PHIL, PLEASE.

© 1989 United Feature Syndicate, Inc.

WHAT'S MY PENALTY? ETERNAL DAMNATION?

I'M JUST GOING TO "DARN YOU" FOR FIFTEEN MINUTES.

IF THE WAREHOUSE WON'T REPLACE MY BROKEN CHAIR, I'LL JUST TAKE ONE FROM SOMEBODY. ELSE.

S.Adams

TECHNICALLY, IT'S NOT STEALING BECAUSE THE CHAIR BELONGS TO THE COMPANY EITHER WAY.

© 1993 United Feature Syndicate, Inc.

12-9

WHAT'S THE WORST THING THAT COULD HAPPEN?

HOLD THE ELEVATOR. ...OVER.

There's that cape again! And I forgot the spoon!

171

IT'S "PHIL, THE PRINCE OF INSUFFICIENT LIGHT"!

I SAW YOU TAKE THAT CHAIR.

I SUMMON ALL THE DEMONS AND TROLLS OF HECK TO COME FORTH AND PUNISH YOU NOW!!!

I'M ED, FROM ACCOUNTING. THE OTHERS ARE AT LUNCH.

I even forgot to make his tail unpointy.

I CAN'T DECIDE IF I SHOULD STAY WITH ENGINEERING OR PURSUE A CAREER IN MANAGEMENT.

IN MY HEART I'M AN ENGINEER BUT I HEAR A VOICE CALLING ME TO THE DARK SIDE.

I FOUND YOUR PROBLEM.

BOY IS MY FACE RED.

A <u>lot</u> of readers were confused by this strip. They hadn't seen Phil for a long time and the spoon was drawn so poorly it wasn't recognizable.

COME TO THE DARK SIDE, DILBERT. RENOUNCE ENGINEERING AND BECOME A MANAGER.

NEVER!!

YOUR TECHNICAL KNOWLEDGE IS GETTING STALE. YOU'RE BECOMING A GENERALIST... TAKE THE EASY PATH.

I BROUGHT YOU A SUITE OF APPLICATIONS THAT ALL WORK TOGETHER.

THAT'S UNNATURAL!!! BE GONE!!!

Here I was using a computer font for lettering, which is a minor sin itself.

HE SLIPS IN LIKE A PANTHER TO TAKE THE LAST CUP OF COFFEE AND NOT MAKE MORE.

I AM PHIL, THE PRINCE OF INSUFFICIENT LIGHT! I DARN YOU TO HECK!!!

PHIL?

YOU WERE ALWAYS MOM'S GOLDEN BOY.

SOMEBODY BROUGHT POTATO SALAD. GIVE ME YOUR SPOON.

Phil's jowl lines have disappeared, just as the boss's did.

MOM WANTED ME TO BE A MANAGER LIKE YOU. BUT I CHOSE MY OWN PATH.

I BECAME PHIL, THE RULER OF HECK, THE PUNISHER OF MINOR SINS!

HOW DO YOU MAKE MONEY?

CORPORATE SPONSORSHIP. "PROCTER AND GAMBLE" PAYS ME TO STAY AWAY FROM THEM.

YOU SHOULD SELL A LINE OF HOME-EXERCISE SPOONS.

The brothers have a reunion.

THIS IS PHIL, RULER OF HECK, WITH A SPECIAL OFFER FOR MY PATENTED "EXERSPOON."

YOU CAN DO OVER SEVEN MILLION EXERCISES WITH THE "EXERSPOON." IT EVEN TRIMS PROBLEM AREAS!

AND THANKS TO THE INNOVATIVE SPOON SHAPE, STORAGE IS A BREEZE!

MMM...

I argued with my editor that nobody would think this cartoon is → **173** → obscene.

Asok is named after a friend of mine from Pacific Bell. A more common spelling is Ashok.

I remember my own gradual increase in awareness about the work world.

I spelled "Jeffries" tube wrong. I was guessing.

Asok, pronounced ah-shook, was introduced to satisfy the hordes of interns who wrote to request their own character. Asok is brilliant, but as an intern he is immensely naive about the cruelties and politics of the business world. The regular cast members have fun at his expense, as is common with most interns.

Asok is from India, but I haven't mentioned that in the strip yet. Only the name gives it away. Prior to Asok, I had intentionally avoided any racial diversity in the primary cast because I only like characters who have huge, gaping character flaws. The world is far too sensitive to let me get away with a highly flawed minority member.

Asok was a good way to tiptoe into the diversity water and test the temperature. Asok's only flaw is his lack of experience, which is obviously temporary. That's as cautious as you can get. But predictably, I have been flamed to a crisp for my alleged "negative stereotype of people from India."

I'm keeping Asok, flames and all. And if I get any more complaints I think I'll turn him into a drug smuggler. I've never been good at playing defense.

Men _do_ have an instinct about unnecessary work. It only _looks_ like we're lazy.

Fortunately, my publishers think this is funny.

Panel 1:
IT HAS COME TO MY ATTENTION THAT 40% OF YOUR SICK DAYS ARE ON FRIDAYS AND MONDAYS. THIS IS UNACCEPTABLE.

Panel 2:
HA HA HA !!! THAT'S A GOOD ONE !!!

Panel 3:
PLEASE TELL ME HE WAS KIDDING.

WELCOME TO HELL, KID.

Probably half of the people who read this didn't realize 40% is exactly normal. Others thought I didn't realize it.

Panel 4:
MY IDEA IS THAT EVERYONE SHOULD BE REQUIRED TO USE SMALL FONTS. THAT WAY WE'LL SAVE DISK SPACE.

Panel 5:
AND I'VE NOTICED THAT MANY PEOPLE USE ENTIRE COLONS IN SITUATIONS WHERE A SEMICOLON WOULD DO JUST FINE.

Panel 6:
YOU'RE RIGHT. THAT WAS FUN.

THE REAL FUN IS WHEN HE DESCRIBES HIS NEW IDEAS AT THE NEXT STAFF MEETING.

Some readers did tests and found out that small fonts _do_ save space, but not much.

Panel 7:
I AM ONLY A LOWLY INTERN, BUT I SEE AN OBVIOUS SOLUTION TO YOUR PROBLEM.

Panel 8:
JUST CLICK HERE... CLEAR YOUR BUFFERS AND INITIALIZE THE LINK... NOW USE THIS CODE PATCH FOR THE MEMORY LEAK.

Panel 9:
THIS IS FUNNY IF YOU CONSIDER THAT YOUR SALARY IS TWICE AS MUCH AS MINE.

I'M LAUGHING ON THE INSIDE.

Tina the Technical Writer

Tina the Technical Writer Do you know anyone who takes personal offense at everything you say, even if you're talking about the weather? I do. That's why I created Tina—to vent some of my frustration at people like that. I labeled her "brittle" as a shorthand for her tendency to be easily offended.

I wanted some gender balance in the strip so I made Tina female. And in order for Tina to fit into Dilbert's office I needed to give her a job. So I made her a Technical Writer. (The job involves translating technical jargon into clear writing for instruction manuals, technical reports, and that sort of thing. Most engineering offices have at least one Technical Writer.)

When Tina first appeared in the strip my e-mail turned into a river of flame. Technical Writers blasted me for maligning their profession. Women and men alike blasted me for what many considered a negative stereotype of women.

I knew I had a winner here.

I was fascinated by the accusations that Tina was a "too stereotypical" female character. It raises a couple of interesting questions:

1. Who says "brittle" is a female stereotype?

2. Is it possible to create a nonstereotypical character?

179

Apparently there's a list of stereotypes somewhere and under the female column is the word "brittle." I was unaware of this list. I can't say it squares with my own observations.

My mother was my most formative female influence. She was born of farmer stock. Mom could put a bullet through a deer's forehead at 300 yards, and did. In fact, she kept a loaded rifle behind the kitchen door to blast bunny rabbits that ventured near our garden. When she wasn't gunning down innocent mammals she was hitting baseballs to my brother and me, or beating us in tennis, or tooling around on her motorcycle.

So what is this "brittle" thing I keep hearing about?

Okay, let's say the critics are right and Tina is "too stereotypical." That brings us to the next question. What would a nonstereotypical character be like? As someone from China once warned: "Be careful what you wish for. You might get it."

Just to stir up trouble, I created Antina (the ANtidote to TINA). Antina didn't dress like a stereotypical woman, didn't talk like a stereotypical woman, didn't have a body like a stereotypical woman, and didn't have stereotypical female interests.

My e-mail caught on fire again. This time I was accused of making fun of lesbians. Obviously there was no safe ground in this game.

After I had my fun I got rid of Antina—she was a one joke character—but I kept Tina and will be broadening her personality over time. That's the only antidote to accusations of stereotyping, but it takes awhile to get there.

TINA, YOU'LL HAVE TO HAVE ALL THE DOCUMENTATION WRITTEN BY NEXT WEEK SO WE CAN SHIP IT WHEN THE SOFTWARE IS DONE.

HOW CAN I WRITE INSTRUCTIONS FOR SOMETHING THAT DOESN'T EXIST YET?

YOU'LL HAVE TO MAKE LOGICAL GUESSES.

"IF YOU PRESS ANY KEY YOUR COMPUTER WILL LOCK UP. IF YOU CALL OUR TECH SUPPORT WE'LL BLAME 'MICROSOFT.'"

It's common to write documentation for things that don't yet exist. As you might guess, it's frustrating.

I FEEL LIKE TWEAKING SOME BRITTLE PEOPLE. DO YOU KNOW ANY BRITTLE PEOPLE?

TRY TINA THE TECH WRITER. SHE BELIEVES THAT ALL FORMS OF EXPRESSION ARE AN INSULT TO HER GENDER AND HER PROFESSION.

THE STATUE OF "VENUS DE MILO" HAS NO ARMS.

OH, I GET IT. YOU'RE SAYING THAT WOMEN CAN'T LIFT HEAVY OBJECTS.

I figured I was wading into dangerous water here.

DOGBERT TWEAKS TINA THE BRITTLE TECH WRITER.

WHAT DO YOU THINK OF THE MOVIE "THELMA AND LOUISE"?

I KNOW WHAT YOU'RE TRYING TO SAY. YOU THINK ALL WOMEN ARE BAD DRIVERS. THAT'S REALLY THE POINT OF THE MOVIE, ISN'T IT??

IF YOU'RE NOT OFFENDED YET, TUNE IN TOMORROW.

THE "THREE STOOGES"?

WHY ARE ALL OF THE DOCUMENTARIES ABOUT MEN??!

Controversy is good. That's my motto.

181

DOGBERT TWEAKS TINA THE BRITTLE TECH WRITER

IS TECHNICAL WRITING THE SAME AS WORD PROCESSING?

NO!!!

I AM A HIGHLY SKILLED COMMUNICATIONS PROFESSIONAL! I CAN TAKE JUMBLES OF INERT THOUGHTS AND BRING THEM TO LIFE!!

MY SECRETARY IS RUNNING THE STAFF MEETING. I NEED YOU TO RETYPE THIS ORG CHART.

THE DOCTOR IS IN!

This is a pet peeve of Technical Writers.

THIS WEEK WE INTRODUCED TINA THE BRITTLE TECH WRITER TO THE STRIP. TINA IS DYSFUNCTIONAL LIKE EVERYBODY HERE EXCEPT ME.

RRRR

SEND YOUR OPINIONS BY E-MAIL TO SCOTTADAMS@AOL.COM

IT'S THE ONLY WAY WE CAN LEARN.

RRRR

PICK ONE
_____

A. WOMEN SHOULD ONLY BE PORTRAYED AS LAWYERS AND STARSHIP CAPTAINS.

B. I DON'T HAVE E-MAIL.

C. TINA SHOULD BE TREATED WITH THE SAME DIGNITY AS DILBERT AND WALLY.

D. TAKE AN ART CLASS.

Sadly, choice "D" was very popular.

A WHILE BACK I ASKED FOR OPINIONS ABOUT THIS NEW CHARACTER, "TINA THE BRITTLE TECH WRITER."

RRRR

RESULTS
_____

MOST PEOPLE, INCLUDING NEARLY ALL SELF-DESCRIBED FEMINISTS, SAID KEEP HER. BUT THERE WERE MANY REQUESTS TO ADD "NON-STEREOTYPICAL" FEMALE CHARACTERS FOR BALANCE.

IN THE INTEREST OF BALANCE I GIVE YOU "ANTINA."

IS ANYBODY UP FOR SOME MATH?

HI, I'M ANTINA THE NON-STEREOTYPICAL WOMAN.

THAT COMPUTER MONITOR YOU'RE USING IS SUPPOSED TO BE 17 INCHES. BUT IT'S MORE LIKE 16.5 INCHES.

I TOOK THE COFFEE MACHINE APART JUST FOR FUN— WANT TO SEE?

The hidden joke is that Dilbert's tie is flat by the third frame. I'm not sure what it means.

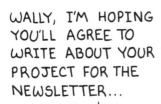

WALLY, I'M HOPING YOU'LL AGREE TO WRITE ABOUT YOUR PROJECT FOR THE NEWSLETTER...

AND IN THE GRAND TRADITION OF ENGINEERING, I EXPECT YOU'LL GIVE THIS THE LOWEST PRIORITY, THUS MAKING ME DESPISE YOU.

SO... ARE YOU SAYING YOU DON'T DESPISE ME NOW?

WE ARE NOT HAVING A "MOMENT" HERE!

Nobody complained that Wally was being a stereotypical male here.

PERFORMANCE REVIEW

YOUR MAIN ACCOMPLISHMENT WAS THE DEPARTMENT NEWSLETTER WHICH WAS BOTH UNINTERESTING AND UNIMPORTANT. YOU GET NO RAISE.

THE NEWSLETTER WAS YOUR IDEA, AND IT'S BORING BECAUSE MOST OF THE ARTICLES ARE CONTRIBUTED BY MY IDIOTIC COWORKERS.

YOU DON'T SEEM TO UNDERSTAND THE VALUE OF TEAM-WORK.

I UNDERSTAND ITS VALUE; IT JUST COST ME A TWO-PERCENT RAISE.

This is another Technical Writer's pet peeve.

DID YOU HEAR THAT THE TINY EAST EUROPEAN COUNTRY OF ELBONIA HAS ABANDONED COMMUNISM?

WHOA! BIG CHANGES AHEAD.

ELBONIA: MONDAY

MUD FARM

ELBONIA: TUESDAY

MY TREE

MY MUD FARM

MY PIG

MY FEET

This was the first glimpse of the Elbonian culture.

THE TINY NATION OF ELBONIA HAS ERUPTED IN CIVIL WAR.

WHAT CAUSED YOU TO TURN YOUR WEAPONS ON YOUR OWN PEOPLE?

WEAPONS? WE CAN USE WEAPONS?

WELL, NO WONDER IT WAS TAKING SO LONG.

I like the idea of an entire country of idiots.

THE PRESIDENT OF ELBONIA ASKED ME TO NEGOTIATE AN END TO THEIR CIVIL WAR.

WHY YOU?

NO DOUBT HE WAS IMPRESSED BY MY DIPLOMACY WHEN I WAS AN ECONOMIC ADVISOR... I JUST WISH I DIDN'T HAVE TO FLY ON ELBONIA AIRLINES.

ELBONIA

...AT HIS WEIGHT, WE CALCULATE THAT ELBONIA AIRLINES WILL FLING HIM RIGHT ON THE REBEL LEADER.

Elbonians Elbonia is an underdeveloped country that comes in handy when I want to involve a foreign location in the strip without hurting my sales of **Dilbert** overseas. People think I have some specific country in mind when I write about Elbonia, but I don't. It represents the view that Americans have of any country that doesn't have cable television—we think they all wear fur hats and wallow around in waist-deep mud.

Some people think the Elbonians are surrounded by snow, but it's mud. I can't color the mud because the Elbonians have shaded clothing and I'd lose the contrast. It's one of those bothersome trade-offs that untalented cartoonists have to make. If you want to think of it as snow, that's okay too.

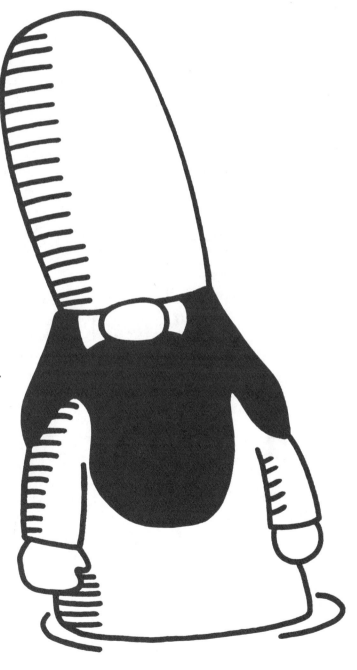

DILBERT TAKES ELBONIA AIRLINES. HE'S BEEN ASKED TO NEGOTIATE AN END TO THE ELBONIAN CIVIL WAR.

I CAN SUCCEED IF I FIND SOME WAY TO IMPRESS THE REBEL LEADER THEY CALL "THE FOX."

THE FOX IS DEAD!!

YOU CRUSHED OUR LEADER. NOW YOU MUST BE THE NEW REBEL LEADER.

I'M A DIPLOMAT, ON A PEACE MISSION.

A WISE ELBONIAN ONCE SAID "IN A RACE BETWEEN A ROCK AND A PIG, DON'T VARNISH YOUR CLAMS."

THAT'S STUPID.

WHAT KIND OF DIPLOMAT ARE YOU??

FIRST DAY ON THE JOB... GIMME A BREAK.

Engineers would not be good diplomats.

WE LEFT-HANDED ELBONIANS HAVE BEEN PERSECUTED FOR CENTURIES. WE MUST CRUSH THE RIGHTIES!

DON'T YOU SEE THAT IT'S ONLY AN ARBITRARY DISTINCTION? ISN'T IT OBVIOUS THAT PEOPLE ARE THE SAME NO MATTER WHAT HAND THEY FAVOR?

NO, THAT ISN'T OBVIOUS TO US AT ALL.

GEEZ, YOU LEFTIES ARE THICK. I'M GLAD I'M NORMAL.

ELBONIANS HEAR ME! YOU MUST END YOUR FUTILE CIVIL WAR.

YOU'VE BEEN LOVING YOUR ANIMALS AND FIGHTING EACH OTHER. A CIVILIZED COUNTRY SHOULD SLAUGHTER THE ANIMALS AND SIMPLY DISCRIMINATE ECONOMICALLY AGAINST EACH OTHER!

© 1992 United Feature Syndicate, Inc.

S. Adams

HOW DID MY SPEECH GO OVER?

I'M SOLD, BUT I THINK THE SECRETARY OF STATE WAS A BIT PUT OFF.

11-24

I'll take any excuse to draw animals.

IN A WAY, I'M GLAD THE ELBONIANS RUN THIS COMPANY NOW.

AFTER YEARS OF BEING THE ONLY FEMALE ENGINEER I'LL ENJOY WATCHING THE ELBONIANS DISCRIMINATE AGAINST YOU GUYS.

S. Adams

3-27 © 1995 United Feature Syndicate, Inc. (NYC)

CONTINUED...

I DIDN'T REALIZE YOU HAD COFFEE WENCHES IN THIS COUNTRY TOO.

I HOPE YOU DON'T WANT CHILDREN, YORGI.

IN THIS COUNTRY WE HAVE A CUSTOM WHEN MEN ASK WOMEN TO FETCH COFFEE.

STAND UP... THAT'S IT... NOW THIS WILL REALLY SURPRISE YOU.

OH GOD

S. Adams

3-28 © 1995 United Feature Syndicate, Inc. (NYC)

I'VE NEVER SEEN ANYBODY GET KICKED INTO HIS HAT BEFORE.

THAT'S GOTTA HURT.

I got complaints for using God's name in vain. I maintain it **187** is a prayer.

In 1989, the boss was tall, thin, and not so pointy-haired.

The Pointy-Haired Boss (PHB) has no other name.

That's intentional. You can more easily imagine him to be your own boss if he has no name.

The original boss had jowls and nonpointy hair. He looked meaner and gruffer that way, but over time his looks and his personality evolved. Now he's more noncaring than he is overtly mean, and more clueless than gruff.

PHB's hair became pointier over time. It started as a gradual change that had no real purpose. One day I noticed it was getting pointier and I liked it. So I decided to go with it and push the hair toward full-blown, demonic horns. It fits his personality perfectly.

WELL, DILBERT, YOU SEEM QUALIFIED FOR THIS PROMOTION, BUT I HAVE ONE CONCERN. SINCE YOUR WORK WOULD BE EVALUATED BY MANY PEOPLE...

9-21   S.Adams

CAN YOU HANDLE CRITICISM?

OH, EASILY. FOR EXAMPLE, YOUR TOUPEE LOOKS LIKE A MULE-STOMPED GOPHER...

© 1989 United Feature Syndicate, Inc.

...TURNS OUT IT WAS A TRICK QUESTION.

BOY, YOU CAN'T TRUST THOSE BALD GUYS.

DILBERT®
By Scott Adams

DILBERT, THE BOSS WOULD LIKE TO TALK TO YOU.

YOU WANTED ME?

AH, DILBERT, COME IN.

I'M TAKING TWO WEEKS OF VACATION AND I NEED COMPETENT LEADERSHIP WHILE I'M GONE.

AT LAST HE'S GIVING ME AN ASSIGNMENT WITH RESPONSIBILITY.

THAT'S WHY I GOT THIS TALKING SOCK MONKEY.

PULL THE STRING TWICE A DAY AND DO WHAT HE SAYS.

12-3   S.Adams

I have a sock monkey. They're great. You should get one.

DILBERT

By Scott Adams

THE WORST HE CAN DO IS FIRE ME...

BOSS, I NEED TO TALK TO YOU.

I FEEL YOU DON'T RESPECT ME...

IT'S AN INTANGIBLE THING...

SNEEZE COMING...

I SEE IT IN YOUR BODY LANGUAGE...

AAH...

...AND SOMETIMES THE THINGS YOU SAY...

RRRRIIP

CHOOO

THIS HAS BEEN SOMETHING LESS THAN A VICTORY FOR WORKERS EVERYWHERE.

He's not sadistic, just uncaring.

ON MY RECENT BUSINESS TRIP TO JAPAN, I LEARNED THAT JAPANESE WORKERS DRESS AS THEIR FAVORITE ANIMALS TO BOOST PRODUCTIVITY.

JAPAN

HA HA HA HA HA

OOH-OOH... AND REMEMBER THE TIME WE TOLD THEM WE ALL DO CALISTHENICS?!

There was a time when all we talked about is how things were done in Japan. I think some of what they did was just pranks on us.

I'VE DECIDED TO REPLACE YOUR DEPART- MENT WITH MACHINES.

YOUR JOB WILL BE FILLED BY THIS LITTLE BIRD THAT BOBS HIS HEAD UP AND DOWN.

... THEN I SAID "HA! IT WOULD TAKE AT LEAST THREE OF THOSE BIRDS TO DO MY JOB!"

IT'S PAY DAY.

HA HA!! DANCE FOR YOUR PAY CHECK!! HA HA HA!! MINE IS TWICE AS BIG!!

AND THEY SAY MONEY CAN'T BUY HAPPINESS.

Jowls .... No Jowls .... Jowls

This became one of the most popular strips I've done.

Humor is relative.

Here he's still in his "cruel" phase.

It must be frustrating to be a boss and not have the option of hurting employees.

This is based closely on real life, except for the fighting.

This was another huge hit. Most employees have been in a meeting like that.

I like to have the characters do the things I would want to do in their position.

I got complaints from Temp agencies.

I NEED TO IDENTIFY ANY UNNECESSARY AND UNPRODUCTIVE EMPLOYEES SO I CAN CUT COSTS.

DOES ANYBODY HAVE SPARE TIME TO JOIN MY TASK FORCE ON PRODUCTIVITY?

10-26

GOOD, GOOD... ANYBODY ELSE?

© 1993 United Feature Syndicate, Inc.

I BORROWED A JAPANESE WORK CUSTOM — SLEEPING TUBES!

NO MORE WASTED TIME COMMUTING. IF YOU KEEL OVER FROM EXHAUSTION WE'LL JUST CRAM YOU INTO A SLEEP TUBE.

© 1993 United Feature Syndicate, Inc.

WHICH TUBE IS MINE?

YOU DON'T GET A PERSONAL TUBE UNLESS YOU'RE EMPLOYEE OF THE WEEK.

11-1

I wonder why this never caught on in the United States.

MY BOSS SAYS WE NEED SOME EUNUCH PROGRAMMERS.

I THINK HE MEANS UNIX NOT EUNUCHS. AND I ALREADY KNOW UNIX.

11-9

© 1993 United Feature Syndicate, Inc.

IF THE COMPANY NURSE DROPS BY, TELL HER I SAID "NEVER MIND."

A huge frustration for technology workers is the imbecile boss.

"TIM WILL BE LEAVING THE COMPANY TO PURSUE OTHER OPPORTUNITIES."

NOTE THE ABSENCE OF KEY PHRASES SUCH AS "WE REGRET" OR "YEARS OF DEDICATED SERVICE." AND NOTICE THAT HIS NEW OPPORTUNITY IS NOT CALLED "EXCITING."

© 1993 United Feature Syndicate, Inc.

1-7-94

I THINK YOU'RE READING A LITTLE TOO MUCH INTO THAT ANNOUNCEMENT.

NO, I'M READING THE FOOTNOTE

I drew this left-handed because I was having hand problems. The lettering gives it away.

YOU'VE COMPLETELY ELIMINATED THE BUDGET FOR TECHNICAL TRAINING!

I'M GETTING DUMBER EVERY MINUTE. MY BRAIN IS STARTING TO SHRIVEL LIKE A RAISIN!

© 1994 United Feature Syndicate, Inc.

2-25

GET OUT OF MY OFFICE.

EVEN MY HAIR FEELS DIFFERENT.

The boss's hair has become a symbol for clueless management.

I CAN ASSURE YOU THAT THE VALUE OF THE AVERAGE EMPLOYEE WILL CONTINUE TO INCREASE.

IS THAT BECAUSE THERE WILL BE LESS OF US, DOING MORE WORK?

© 1994 United Feature Syndicate, Inc.

3-9

I'M RIGHT, AREN'T I?

EXCEPT FOR THE "US" PART.

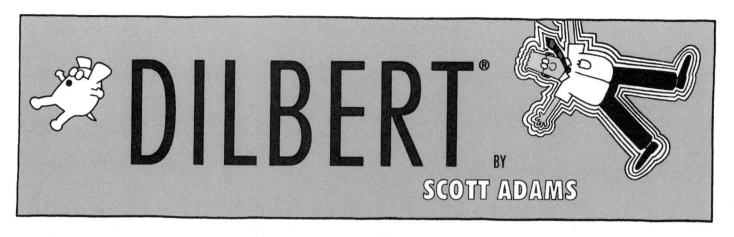

HERE'S YOUR EMPLOYEE LOCATOR DEVICE.

SENSORS IN THE BUILDING WILL BE ABLE TO TRACK YOU AT ALL TIMES.

WE'LL KNOW HOW MANY TIMES YOU USE THE RESTROOM AND HOW LONG.

IT'S A DOG COLLAR... THE FINAL HUMILIATION.

ONCE YOU GOT USED TO WORKING IN CUBICLES, LIKE GERBILS, WE KNEW ANYTHING WAS POSSIBLE.

MY CONFORMANCE RATIONALIZATION MECHANISMS ARE KICKING IN.

IT'S NOT SO BAD. A COLLAR IS SIMPLY AN EFFICIENT DESIGN. EVERYONE IS DOING IT.

2-27

IT'S NOT SO BAD.

IT'S POWERED BY THIS SIX FOOT LONG EXTENSION CORD.

Employees can get used to anything.

This explains most levels of management.

This is the peak of pointiness, hair-wise.

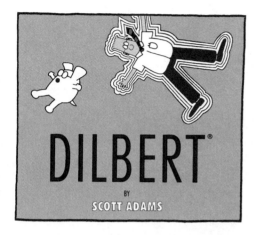

DILBERT

BY SCOTT ADAMS

HI, GUYS. HOW ARE YOUR FAMILIES?

?   ?

WHY ARE YOU PRETENDING TO BE INTERESTED IN OUR PERSONAL LIVES?

IT'S A MANAGEMENT TECHNIQUE TO INCREASE YOUR JOB SATISFACTION WITHOUT GIVING YOU MORE MONEY.

MY PLAN IS TO BOOST YOUR INTANGIBLE BENEFITS WHILE CONTINUING TO CHISEL AWAY AT YOUR SALARIES.

5-15

BUT ENOUGH ABOUT ME... HOW ARE THOSE FAMILIES OF YOURS?

MY WIFE DIVORCED ME BECAUSE YOU MAKE ME WORK SO MANY HOURS.

THIS JOB LOWERS MY SELF-ESTEEM TOO MUCH TO ATTRACT A MATE.

TELL THEM I SAID "HI."

I had a boss who tried this technique on me, with similar success.

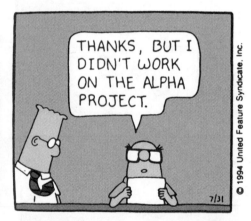

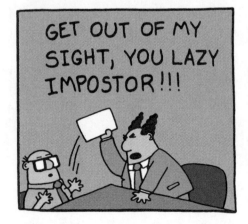

I hate this cartoon. 202 I was tired.

THIS WILL BE A TOUGH YEAR FOR THE COMPANY.

IT WILL TAKE A SPECIAL KIND OF TEAM TO GET BY.

GO TEAM!

TEAM! TEAM!

YES!

SPECIFICALLY, IT WILL TAKE A MUCH SMALLER TEAM.

© 1994 United Feature Syndicate, Inc.

Do you remember when everyone was on the same side?

WE'LL BE GETTING A NEW "BUNGEE BOSS" SOMETIME TODAY.

HI-I'M-YOUR-NEW-BOSS-LET'S-CHANGE-EVERY-THING-BEFORE-I-GET-REASSIGNED-OOPS-TOO-LATE-GOODBYE.

SPROING

HE WAS LIKE A MENTOR TO ME.

I THINK HE MADE A DIFFERENCE.

INCOMING!

© 1994 United Feature Syndicate, Inc.

This strip was so popular that the phrase "Bungee Boss" has entered the vocabulary at some companies.

WORK HARDER OR I'LL HAVE YOU PUT IN THE "BOX."

REALLY? I THOUGHT I WAS ALREADY IN THE BOX.

IS THE BOX BIGGER THAN MY CUBICLE?

THESE PEOPLE ARE TOTALLY UNMANAGE-ABLE.

© 1994 United Feature Syndicate, Inc.

I'M RUNNING LATE. BUT SINCE I'M A VICE PRESIDENT YOU'LL HAVE TO WAIT IN THE HALLWAY.

YOU'LL BE ABLE TO JUDGE YOUR RELATIVE WORTH BY OBSERVING WHAT THINGS I DO WHILE YOU WAIT.

HE'S TEACHING HIMSELF THE BANJO.

© 1994 United Feature Syndicate, Inc.

9-27

I waited in a lot of hallways at Pacific Bell.

THIS CARTOON SEEMS TO BE SAYING THAT MANAGEMENT DECISIONS ARE A JOKE.

CARTOONS ARE NOT ALLOWED ON CUBICLES. IT HURTS MORALE. I DON'T WANT TO SEE THIS WHEN I RETURN.

9-28

I'VE NOTICED A REAL IMPROVEMENT IN MORALE SINCE YOU REMOVED THE CARTOON.

© 1994 United Feature Syndicate, Inc.

I'm constantly hearing about employees getting in trouble for putting Dilbert cartoons on their cubicles.

THIS LAPTOP COMPUTER WEIGHS TOO MUCH. DO WE HAVE ANYTHING LIGHTER?

WHY DON'T YOU JUST DELETE FILES TO LOWER THE WEIGHT ON THAT ONE?

© 1995 United Feature Syndicate, Inc.

1-30

THAT'S A THOUGHT.

TECHNICALLY, I ONLY ASKED WHY NOT.

Somewhere, you know someone has tried this.

BOSS TYPES

FIND YOUR BOSS ON THIS HANDY REFERENCE.

HOSTAGE TAKER: TRAPS YOU IN YOUR CUBICLE AND TALKS YOUR EARS OFF.

BLAH BLAH

OW!!

FRAUD: USES VIGOROUS HEAD-NODDING TO SIMULATE COMPREHENSION.

THEN WE'LL SUBNET OUR IP ADDRESSES.

OH YEAH OH YEAH

MOTIVATIONAL LIAR: HAS NO CLUE WHAT YOU DO BUT SAYS YOU'RE THE BEST.

NOBODY CAN DO WHAT YOU DO!!

EXCEPT A MUSHROOM.

OVER PROMOTED: TRIES TO MASK INCOMPETENCE WITH POOR COMMUNICATION.

LET'S QUALITIZE OUR PARADIGM SO WE DON'T OVER INUNDATE WITH DATUMS.

WEASEL: TAKES CREDIT FOR YOUR HARD WORK.

THIS BONUS IS FOR BRILLIANTLY FORCING YOUR STAFF TO WORK 80 HOUR WEEKS.

IT WASN'T EASY!

MOSES: PERPETUALLY WAITS FOR CLEAR SIGNALS FROM ABOVE.

DON'T DO ANYTHING IMPORTANT YET.

NEVER HAVE.

PERFECT BOSS: DIES OF NATURAL CAUSES ON A THURSDAY AFTERNOON.

SHOULD WE DO SOMETHING?

THREE DAY WEEKEND!

Do any of these look familiar?

This — by far — is the most popular cartoon I've ever drawn.

↰ That's based on reality.

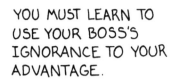
YOU MUST LEARN TO USE YOUR BOSS'S IGNORANCE TO YOUR ADVANTAGE.

FIND OUT WHAT IMPRESSES HIM AND LIST IT ON YOUR ACCOMPLISHMENTS.

YOU'RE THE ACTOR IN THE "BARNEY" SUIT?!! I LOVE THAT GUY!

DON'T TELL ANYBODY MY SECRET IDENTITY.

I'VE DECIDED TO BE MORE OF A HANDS-ON MANAGER.

MOVE THE MOUSE...UP... UP... OVER... MORE... NOW CLICK IT!! CLICK IT!!

NO!!! YOU FOOL!!!

THIS HAS "LONG DAY" WRITTEN ALL OVER IT.

A phrase you never want to hear is "hands-on manager."

HEY! THAT LITTLE STUFFED DOLL LOOKS JUST LIKE ME!

IT GIVES ME AN EMOTIONAL LIFT TO HAVE YOUR LIKENESS NEARBY.

I NEVER REALIZED WHAT HE THOUGHT OF ME.

STOP DROPPING IN LIKE THAT!!

WHACK!

So many people asked for a boss doll after this came out that we made one. **207**

ALICE BROUGHT HER NEW BABY TO THE OFFICE TODAY.

WHAT ARE YOU SUPPOSED TO SAY WHEN SOMEBODY SHOWS YOU A BABY?

"PRECIOUS" USUALLY WORKS.

JUDGING FROM THE REACTION, "BUG-UGLY" WASN'T WHAT SHE WAS LOOKING FOR.

5-20
S.Adams

This was the first appearance of Alice. She didn't have the distinct attitude she has now.

WHEN'S THE BABY DUE?

ANY MINUTE NOW.

THIS COMPANY HAS NO MATERNITY LEAVE POLICY, SO I'M GOING TO DELIVER BY THE XEROX MACHINE AND KEEP WORKING.

8-5

THAT DOESN'T SEEM FAIR.

YEAH, ESPECIALLY IF YOU NEED TO MAKE COPIES.

The "xerox" machine is a good place to reproduce.

ALICE, I NOTICED YOU GAVE BIRTH BY THE XEROX MACHINE THIS MORNING...

WE DON'T HAVE A MATER- NITY LEAVE POLICY HERE, BUT IF YOU NEED SOME TIME, I'M SURE WE CAN FIND SOMEBODY LESS FERTILE TO FILL YOUR JOB.

THANK YOU, SIR, BUT I DON'T EXPECT ANY SPECIAL TREATMENT.

8-6

I had a long discussion with my editor about this one.

Alice wasn't always Alice. In the beginning there were a variety of fluffy-haired female characters in Dilbert's office but they didn't have many lines. Over time the personality of my friend and co-worker at Pacific Bell started to channel into the strip, emerging as the recurring character Alice. Alice's real-world counterpart (actual name Anita) was the model for Alice's pink suit, her fluffy hair, her long work hours, her coffee obsession, her technical proficiency, and her take-no-crap attitude.

As far as I know, the human version of Alice has never kicked a man into his hat, stuffed an intern into his shirt sleeve, or slapped a man so hard he traveled back in time. But if I ever hear about it happening, it won't surprise me.

Alice's hair has become bigger and more triangular for no real reason except that I like it that way. It's a challenge to keep it in the frame sometimes but it's worth it.

This is a suggestion of the Alice to come.

← I stuck Dilbert here so you'd know what comic you were reading.

This was a generic Alice-like character.

ALICE, MARY, LET'S GO TO THE LADIES ROOM!

I RENTED "GONE WITH THE WIND." WE CAN WATCH IT ON THE BIG SCREEN TV

I WANT THE GREY SOFA!

HEY, LOOK! THE MEN'S ROOM HAS SOAP!!

AS PART OF MY PROGRAM TO USE MORE HUMOR AT WORK, I'M ASKING EACH OF YOU TO WEAR A "KICK ME" SIGN.

I'LL CHECK LATER TO SEE IF YOU'RE MORE RELAXED AND CREATIVE.

LATER...

YOU SEEM TO BE TAKING UNFAIR ADVANTAGE OF THE SITUATION, ALICE...

This is a cheap laugh, but I'm not proud.

LET'S START WITH A BRAINSTORMING EXERCISE. ALICE, YOU GO FIRST.

I IMAGINE MYSELF NOT SURROUNDED BY DULL, UNATTRACTIVE, AND LARGELY CLUELESS MEN.

I THINK SHE JUST INSULTED YOU GUYS.

MMMM...

It's tough to be the only woman in engineering.

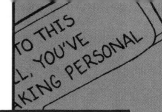

Alice's personality is becoming fully formed at this point.

She's overworked, so she has a reason to be cranky.

I'M PROTESTING THE COMPANY'S DRESS CODE. I REFUSE TO DRESS LIKE A WOMAN.

HIGH HEELS AND PANTYHOSE ARE DESIGNED TO MAKE WOMEN LOOK LIKE HELPLESS LITTLE ORNAMENTS FOR THE PLEASURE OF MALE VIEWERS!

I'VE NEVER HAD PLEASURE VIEWING YOU. I SWEAR.

THANK YOU FOR YOUR SUPPORT.

The hair has taken a vaguely pyramid shape.

I'M DRESSING LIKE A MAN TO PROTEST THE COMPANY'S DRESS CODE.

SO, WHAT YOU'RE SAYING IS THAT YOU'RE ACTUALLY A WOMAN. IS THAT YOUR CLAIM?

THAT'S NOT EXACTLY THE POINT.

I SAW "THE CRYING GAME." DON'T DO ANYTHING THAT WOULD MAKE ME HEAVE.

WHEN YOU CONSIDER THE HOURS I WORK, I MAKE LESS PER HOUR THAN THE JANITOR!

2/10

LOOK WHAT WAS BLOCKING THE PIPES! IT TOOK ME ALL MORNING TO PLUNGE THE RASCAL OUT.

I LOVE MY JOB.

I'M GIVING HIM A RAISE.

↰ I don't know what that is.

213

I've noticed that women care about their performance reviews far more than men do. (Yeah, I know it's an unfair generalization.)

This explains it.

No matter how good a performance review is, it's never good enough.

I'D LIKE TO KICK-OFF THE PROJECT WITH THE TRADITIONAL BAD-MOUTHING OF THE GUY WHO WORKED ON THIS BEFORE.

HE'S SO SLIMY THAT SLUGS POUR SALT ON HIM. HIS BRAIN WOULD RATTLE IN A FLEA'S SKULL!

OH, AND I'LL NEED YOUR FILES.

FLEAS DON'T HAVE "SKULLS"!!

This tradition will live forever.

ALICE IS SITTING IN FOR THE BOSS!

PRODUCTIVITY AT LAST !!!

EFFICIENCY! YES!!

AS LONG AS SHE DOESN'T GET AN ATTITUDE...

ALICE SITS IN FOR THE BOSS

I WILL APPROVE YOUR EXPENSE VOUCHER ON ONE CONDITION.

YOU MUST SLAY THE CREATURE WHO STALKS THE OFFICE AT NIGHT AND EATS OUR HIDDEN SNACKS!!!

IT HAS TO BE EITHER YOU OR THE SECURITY GUARD.

SLAY HIM FIRST AND SEE IF THE PROBLEM STOPS.

This is just a mouse, not Ratbert.

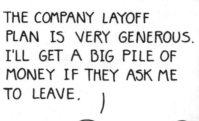

UH... WALLY, YOU'RE WEARING ONLY UNDERWEAR AT WORK.

I'M TRYING TO GET FIRED.

THE COMPANY LAYOFF PLAN IS VERY GENEROUS. I'LL GET A BIG PILE OF MONEY IF THEY ASK ME TO LEAVE.

THIS HAS GIVEN ME A DEGREE OF FREEDOM IN DEALING WITH LOCAL MANAGEMENT.

Wally is always trying to work the system.

WHAT'S THE STORY WITH THE COSTUME, WALLY?

THE BOSS PUT ME ON A SPECIAL TASK FORCE TO SEE IF HUMOR INCREASES CREATIVITY. I HAVE TO DRESS LIKE THIS FOR A MONTH.

ARE YOU FEELING MORE CREATIVE?

YEAH. I'VE ALREADY THOUGHT OF SIX HUNDRED WAYS TO KILL HIM.

This was inspired by a woody Allen movie where woody played a court jester. I liked the look.

HEY, WALLY, HOW DID YOU GET A ROOF FOR YOUR CUBICLE?

THIS STUFF IS ALL MODULAR. YOU JUST TAKE SOME IDIOT'S WALL AND MAKE IT YOUR CEILING.

BY ANY CHANCE, DO YOU KNOW WHAT HAPPENED TO MY WALL?

WHAT DID IT LOOK LIKE?

There were a number of pre-Wally characters who had similar looks and bit parts in Dilbert's office. The true Wally didn't emerge until one of my co-workers at Pacific Bell found himself in an unusual situation: He wanted to leave the company, but not without getting one of the generous buyout packages that were being offered as part of the larger downsizing efforts. Unfortunately, the buyouts were limited to people who were identified as being in the lowest ten percent of the performers. That created a bizarre incentive for my co-worker to try as hard as he could to become the worst possible employee in order to get money for leaving. This wouldn't have been so fun to watch except that this fellow was one of the more brilliant people I've met and he was totally dedicated to this goal.

I loved the concept of a thoroughly cynical employee who has no sense of company loyalty and feels no need to mask his poor performance or his total lack of respect. Wally was born.

HERE'S YOUR "BUZZWORD BINGO" CARD FOR THE MEETING .

2-22

IF THE BOSS USES A BUZZWORD ON YOUR CARD, YOU CHECK IT OFF. THE OBJECTIVE IS TO FILL A ROW .

S.Adams

© 1994 United Feature Syndicate, Inc.

YOU'RE ALL VERY ATTENTIVE TODAY. MY PROACTIVE LEADERSHIP MUST BE WORKING!

BINGO, SIR .

You can never be sure when Wally is being sarcastic.

Bad things happen to Wally. He takes it in stride.

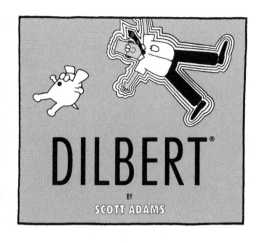

EXHIBIT "A" IS MY EMPTY LUNCH BAG, LAST SEEN FULL.

ONLY THE PEOPLE IN THIS ROOM HAD THE MOTIVE AND THE OPPORTUNITY.

INSPECTOR DOGBERT WILL INVESTIGATE.

SNIFF※ YOU WERE IN THE SUPPLY ROOM WITH WILLY THE MAIL BOY ALL MORNING. YOU ARE INNOCENT.

SORT OF.

SNIFF ※ I GIVE YOU A "C+" FOR HYGIENE BUT YOU DID NOT TAKE THE LUNCH.

SNIFF※ BOLOGNA... POTATO CHIPS... CARROT STICKS... HA !!!

THIS IS THE THIEF WHO TOOK THE DECOY LUNCH... WHICH WE LACED WITH SYNTHETIC FEMALE HORMONES!

10-30

YOU CAN'T PROVE ANYTHING!

IS THERE SOMETHING YOU'D LIKE TO GET OFF YOUR CHEST?

Some women complained because they said I'm implying that being female is a punishment.

That's actually Wally, but it's not obvious.

I've noticed that other people can be inflexible.

DILBERT® BY SCOTT ADAMS

WALLY, YOU NEVER REALLY ANSWERED THE QUESTION I LEFT ON YOUR VOICE-MAIL.

IS THIS A CASE OF SIMPLE INCOMPETENCE OR A PREVIEW OF SOMETHING FAR MORE SINISTER?

IT'S THE SINISTER ONE.

I'VE ADOPTED A DEFENSIVE STRATEGY. I'M WITHHOLDING INFORMATION TO MAKE MYSELF APPEAR MORE VALUABLE.

NOW I ONLY RETURN PHONE CALLS LATE AT NIGHT AND LEAVE INCOMPLETE ANSWERS.

IN PERSON, I ACT OVERWORKED AND IRRATIONAL SO PEOPLE STOP ASKING QUESTIONS.

IF CORNERED, I SIGH DEEPLY AND RECOUNT OLD WAR STORIES THAT DON'T RELATE TO THE QUESTION.

GOT IT!

NO CO-WORKER CAN THWART ME!

WHAT IF THEY TEAM UP?

There's always someone like this in every group. **221**

I spent 17 years in corporate jobs and never did anything that made an impact. I don't think I was alone.

Wally is easy to draw, so he gets a lot of face time.

YOU COULD OFFER FREE REPLACEMENTS FOR ALL THE KEYBOARDS YOU SOLD WITHOUT A "Q," OR YOU COULD BLAME THE MEDIA FOR BLOWING IT OUT OF PROPORTION.

LET'S BLAME THE MEDIA. THEY'LL ADMIT THEY WERE WRONG AND THE WHOLE THING WILL DISAPPEAR.

YOU HAVE A BRILLIANT GRASP OF HUMAN NATURE, WALLY.

I KNOW. MY THIRD WIFE ALWAYS SAID THE SAME THING.

Wally has been married but now he's single.

WE'RE MOVING TO A NEW OFFICE ACROSS TOWN. I VOLUNTEERED TO COORDINATE THE MOVE.

I CONTROL YOUR CUBICLE ASSIGNMENT. NAY, YOUR VERY EXISTENCE. FROM NOW ON YOU WILL REFER TO ME AS "LORD WALLY THE PUPPET MASTER."

I DON'T THINK IT'S LEGAL TO ENJOY YOUR WORK THIS MUCH.

I BANISH YOU TO THE CUBICLE CLOSEST TO YOUR BOSS!!

Wally is the kind of guy who shouldn't have power.

ALLOW ME TO INTRODUCE LOUD HOWARD.

HI!

I WILL MAKE LOUD HOWARD YOUR CUBICLE NEIGHBOR IN THE NEW OFFICE UNLESS YOU GIVE ME YOUR IMMORTAL SOUL!!

NICE DAY!

...FORTUNATELY I CONVINCED HIM TO TAKE MY LASER PRINTER INSTEAD...

WHAT DID I SAY THAT SOUNDED LIKE "TELL ME ABOUT YOUR DAY"?

. . . and Hygiene Issues

DON'T GET TOO CLOSE-- I FOUND OUT THAT MY BALDNESS IS CAUSED BY TOO MUCH TESTOSTERONE.

NOW WITH MY HAIR GONE I'M AFRAID THE TESTOSTERONE WILL START FLINGING OUT OF MY PORES.

HEY! YOU GOT SOME ON MY SHIRT!

DO YOU HAVE A PROBLEM WITH THAT?

I'm glad that baldness is becoming somewhat fashionable.

GEE, WALLY, YOU SURE HAVE BEEN POPULAR WITH WOMEN SINCE THE TESTOSTERONE STARTED SPEWING FROM YOUR HEAD.

IT'S AMAZING ... I EVEN BOUGHT A PICKUP TRUCK AND A RIFLE SO I CAN HUNT AFTER WORK.

WHAT DO YOU HUNT AROUND HERE?

PIGEONS ARE THE MOST CONVENIENT... DON'T EVEN HAVE TO GET OUT OF THE TRUCK.

I GUESS IT'S TIME TO GO BACK TO MY DIMLY LIT CUBICLE AND SEE IF MY CARPAL TUNNEL HAS CRIPPLED ME YET.

THIS IS A LOT LIKE MY LAST JOB AS A COAL MINER, BUT WITHOUT THE THREAT OF A GAS EXPLOSION.

I'M MOVING YOU TO A NEW CUBICLE OVER BY WALLY.

BETTER GET A CANARY.

You see, miners use canaries to sense gas...

I'VE GIVEN UP ON THE WHOLE DATING SCENE. I'VE DECIDED TO REPRODUCE BY ASEXUAL CELL DIVISION.

I DIDN'T REALIZE THAT WAS AN OPTION.

YOU NEVER KNOW UNTIL YOU TRY.

← My motto.

I THINK I'LL STEER CLEAR OF HERE FOR A WHILE.

DIVIDE! DIVIDE!

YOUR IGNORANCE SEEMS TO HAVE NO LIMIT. YOUR OPINIONS ARE IDIOTIC.

YOUR PERSONAL HYGIENE LEAVES MUCH TO BE DESIRED. YOUR FAMILY IS UGLY.

SEND E-MAIL

YOU'RE MIGHTY BRAVE IN CYBERSPACE, FLAME-BOY.

STEP INSIDE.

On the Internet, everyone is a bully.

I WAS SO LATE I HAD TO PUT ON MY MAKEUP IN THE CAR.

YEAH, I HAD TO SHAVE IN THE CAR.

THAT'S NOTHING. I WAS SO LATE THAT I HAD TO GIVE MYSELF A SPONGE BATH IN THE CAR.

AREN'T YOU THE DRIVER FOR YOUR CARPOOL?

YOU'VE NEVER HEARD SUCH WHINING.

"sponge bath" is a good comedy phrase.

I've had big problems with secretaries.

↖ This became a Dilbert book title.

Carol Sometimes you'll find a secretary who likes and respects the boss and is helpful to everyone else in the office. But more often you get the "secretary from hell" who hates her job and finds perverse joy in making everyone within a two-mile radius suffer. Carol is one of the secretaries who tries to get as much of this sadistic joy as possible. She's a composite of all the bad experiences I've ever had with any secretary, and there have been many.

The "secretary with a crossbow" came from an e-mail message from a secretary who said she sometimes wished she had one.

I hear lots of stories of initials that spell words.

HERE'S MY TIME SHEET, FILLED OUT IN INCREMENTS OF FIFTEEN MINUTES.

AS USUAL, I CODED THE USELESS HOURS SPENT IN MEETINGS AS "WORK," WHEREAS THE TIME I SPENT IN THE SHOWER DESIGNING CIRCUITS IN MY MIND IS "NON-WORK."

INTERESTINGLY, EVEN THE TIME I SPEND COMPLAINING ABOUT MY LACK OF PRODUCTIVITY IS CONSIDERED "WORK."

I HATE MY LIFE.

what exactly is "work" for a person who is paid to think?

WE'RE POISED FOR SUCCESS. WE EXPECT HUGE EARNINGS AND INCREASED MARKET SHARE!

NEXT ON THE AGENDA... THERE WILL BE NO RAISES BECAUSE IT WILL BE A DIFFICULT YEAR...

CAROL, I THOUGHT I TOLD YOU TO PUT THE "UNITED WAY" UPDATE BETWEEN THOSE TWO AGENDA ITEMS.

OOPSIE.

Carol's not-so-secret desire is to kill her evil boss.

CAROL, ABOUT THIS FLIGHT TO NEW YORK THAT YOU BOOKED FOR ME...

IS IT REALLY NECESSARY TO MAKE ALL THESE STOPOVERS IN THIRD-WORLD COUNTRIES THAT ARE EXPERIENCING REBEL INSURRECTIONS?

YOU'D BETTER WEAR THE INTERNATIONAL SYMBOL OF THE "RED CROSS" ON YOUR BACK.

YIKES !!! A SKUNK IN THE HOUSE !!!

HI.

OH, DON'T WORRY; WE SKUNKS ONLY SPRAY WHEN WE'RE SCARED... I CERTAINLY WOULDN'T USE MY THREATENING POWER TO FORCE YOU TO DO MY BIDDING.

S.Adams 12-14

THEN WHY IS YOUR TAIL TWITCHING ?!

I'M SCARED YOU MIGHT NOT OFFER ME A BIG BOWL OF STRAWBERRY ICE CREAM.

© 1989 United Feature Syndicate, Inc.

I used to work at a mountain resort where the skunks would walk through the kitchen without fear.

DILBERT IS THREATENED BY AN ABUSIVE SKUNK.

THAT'S RIGHT: A BIG BOWL OF ICE CREAM COULD KEEP ME FROM BEING AFRAID AND REFLEXIVELY SPRAYING YOUR LIVING ROOM.

S.Adams

THIS IS BLACKMAIL!

MY GOODNESS, NO. IT'S JUST THAT I CAN'T CONTROL MY FEAR RESPONSE.

NOW I'M AFRAID THAT YOU WON'T SING THE SONGS FROM "CATS" WHILE I EAT.

© 1989 United Feature Syndicate, Inc. 12-15

DILBERT, GO DOWN TO THE ACCOUNTING DEPARTMENT AND FIND OUT WHAT THESE FIGURES MEAN.

GULP

NO... P-PLEASE... THEY AREN'T EVEN HUMAN THERE !!!

© 1990 United Feature Syndicate, Inc.

S.Adams 8-13

I DON'T LIKE HIM.

SURPRISE.

Some of my worst business experiences involve accounting.

CRITTERS

Miscellaneous Critters Some people remind me of particular animals. I love to substitute the actual animal for human beings in the strip because it sends such a clear message. Everyone understands what I mean when I represent the accounting department as trolls or the marketing guy as a weasel. When Dilbert's blind date turns out to be a literal dog it seems oddly familiar.

Here are some of my favorite strips that feature animals and other strange creatures.

Do any accountants in big companies have good attitudes?

← People who work with numbers start to believe this.

Turtles seem like the dumbest pets to have. Even the "Pet Rock" had funny instructions.

You see, turtles are slow...

This is just like my dinosaur egg joke you saw earlier.

Much of my cubicle jobs could have been done by monkeys.

whenever there was a loud noise, the cubicles looked like prairie dog habitats.

I love the concept of a lazy beaver. But he doesn't fit into the strip.

WHEN YOU'RE A LAZY BEAVER, YOU TRY TO FIND SHORTCUTS AND TRICKS TO GET YOUR WORK DONE.

I GOT THIS DAYTIME PLANNER TO ORGANIZE MY DAY MORE EFFICIENTLY.

BUT ALL IT DOES IS SIT THERE.

LOOKS LIKE YOU GOT A BAD ONE.

I think it's the coffee cup that sells this character.

I'VE GOT TO CUT STAFF IN ENGINEERING. I'M TRYING TO DETERMINE WHICH ONE OF YOU IS MORE VALUABLE TO KEEP.

I'VE BEEN HEARING GOOD THINGS ABOUT ZIMBU THE MONKEY. WHICH ONE OF YOU IS ZIMBU THE MONKEY?

THIS IS NOT THE PROUDEST MOMENT OF MY PROFESSIONAL CAREER.

I made up the name Zimbu because it sounds like a monkey name to me.

ZIMBU THE MONKEY DESIGNED THREE COMMERCIAL PRODUCTS THIS WEEK! WE'D BETTER FIND OUT HIS SECRET.

HE'S USING HIS TAIL! HE HAS A NATURAL ADVANTAGE!

I FEEL THE JAWS OF EVOLUTION ON MY THROAT.

GOOD GRAVY! DID YOU SEE HIM CUT AND PASTE?!

Why don't people have tails?

ZIMBU, YOU'RE NOT SUPPOSED TO USE YOUR TAIL TO OPERATE THE MOUSE.

IF TAILS WERE A NATURAL ADVANTAGE FOR ENGINEERS THEN EVOLUTION WOULD PROVIDE US ALL WITH TAILS!

3-30

DILBERT, I DON'T BELIEVE YOU'VE MET ROCKY, OUR NEW C PROGRAMMER.

I wish I had a tail.

EVOLUTION FAVORS MONKEYS. EVENTUALLY, HUMANS WILL BE KEPT IN CAGES AS PETS...

BAH!

IMPOSSIBLE! WE HUMANS WILL NEVER ALLOW OURSELVES TO BE TREATED LIKE THAT!

4-1

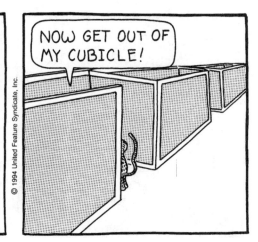

NOW GET OUT OF MY CUBICLE!

Some day we'll look back and be amazed that we put up with cubicles.

TELL ME ABOUT YOUR PROJECT AND I'LL TRANSLATE IT INTO WEASEL WORDS FOR THE BUSINESS CASE.

WELL... AN EXECUTIVE HAD LUNCH WITH A VENDOR AND COMMITTED TO BUY SOME STUFF THAT DOESN'T WORK. OUR JOB IS TO COST-JUSTIFY THE DECISION.

4-13

I QUIT.

DON'T GET ALL ETHICAL ON US.

This used to be my job, but I was less ethical.

OUR CEO CANCELLED HIS VISIT. HE'S SENDING HIS TOP AID, ZIMBU THE MONKEY, IN HIS PLACE.

ISN'T THAT TYPICAL? I SPENT A WEEK EXAGGERATING MY ACCOMPLISHMENTS FOR THIS. NOW HE SENDS A STUPID MONKEY!

WHAT COULD BE MORE HUMILIATING THAN TRYING TO SUCK-UP TO A MONKEY?

FAILING AT IT?

The harder you prepare, the less likely the meeting will happen.

HA HA! NOW THAT THE ENGINEERS MUST CHARGE THEIR TIME TO MARKETING, WE OWN YOU!

I'LL JUST REPROGRAM YOUR COMPUTER THROUGH THE LAN SO ITS RADIATION WILL ALTER YOUR DNA.

IS THAT POSSIBLE??!

AS FAR AS YOU KNOW.

This is the only defense the engineers have.

I TOLD A GUY IN MARKETING THAT I PROGRAMMED HIS COMPUTER TO ALTER HIS DNA STRUCTURE.

HEE HEE

HE THINKS HE'LL TURN INTO SOME KIND OF ANIMAL.

TELL HIM YOU SET IT TO "WEASEL." IT'LL TAKE LONGER TO NOTICE ANY CHANGE.

TELL ME THE TRUTH, ALICE. CAN DILBERT REPROGRAM MY DNA?

YEAH. YOU MARKETING GUYS ONLY HAVE ONE HELIX.

MAYBE YOU SHOULDN'T HAVE TOLD STAN YOU REPROGRAMMED HIS DNA THROUGH THE LAN.

THOSE MARKETING GUYS BELIEVE ANYTHING. THEY EVEN BELIEVE MARKET RESEARCH, FOR HEAVEN'S SAKE.

THERE'S NO TELLING WHAT THE POWER OF SUGGESTION MIGHT DO.

WELL, THANK YOU VERY MUCH.

People would be much cuter if we all had round noses and big whiskers.

I JOKINGLY TOLD STAN IN MARKETING THAT I REPROGRAMMED HIS DNA. HE'S SO GULLIBLE THAT HE'S ACTUALLY CHANGING!

YOU MUST USE HIS GULLIBILITY TO REVERSE THE PROCESS. REMEMBER, HIS ENTIRE REALITY IS SHAPED BY UNVERIFIED CUSTOMER ANECDOTES.

I HEARD A RUMOR OF A STORY OF AN ALLEGED FOCUS GROUP WHERE A QUOTE TAKEN OUT OF CONTEXT INDICATES YOU'RE NOT BECOMING A WEASEL.

I'M NOT?!

YIPEEE!

MY STATUS FOR THE WEEK IS THAT THE ONGOING DEHUMANIZATION FROM MY JOB HAS CAUSED ME TO DOUBT MY EXISTENCE.

THERE IS REASON TO BELIEVE I AM BECOMING INVISIBLE.

DO I HEAR YOUR PAGER BUZZING, WALLY?

I DOUBT IT; I DON'T KEEP BATTERIES IN IT.

PLINK

I've had this feeling.

THE DEHUMANIZATION OF MY JOB HAS RENDERED ME INVISIBLE TO HUMANS. ONLY YOU CAN SEE ME, DOGBERT.

HOW CAN WE FIX THIS?

YOU COULD WEAR A BAG ON YOUR HEAD WHEN YOU'RE AROUND ME.

THAT'S NOT THE FIX I HAD IN MIND.

IT'S NOT A PERFECT SOLUTION. I'D STILL BE ABLE TO HEAR YOU.

The only cure for workplace invisibility is to screw something up.

YOU'RE INVISIBLE TO YOUR CO-WORKERS. BUT YOU CAN COMPENSATE BY FORMING A SYMBIOTIC RELATIONSHIP WITH A VISIBLE CREATURE.

RATBERT WILL CLING TO YOUR BACK. HE'LL BE YOUR VISUAL AND AUDITORY LINK WITH YOUR CO-WORKERS.

SO... WORKING HARD? OR HARDLY WORKING?

I KNEW THIS COLOMBIAN COFFEE WAS TROUBLE.

I got a complaint from a colombian who didn't like the coffee reference.

DON'T BE ALARMED. I'M NOT REALLY A RAT FLOATING IN MIDAIR.

I'M CLINGING TO THE BACK OF AN EMPLOYEE WHO HAS BEEN RENDERED INVISIBLE BY A LONG SUCCESSION OF WORTHLESS ASSIGNMENTS.

LOOKS LIKE AN ISOLATED CASE OF BAD ATTITUDE.

WHICH ROOM IS THE "QUALITY" MEETING IN?

I'm always shy in restaurants.

DOGBERT

Dogbert in Hats There are few things in life that are as funny as a dog in a hat. Since Dogbert doesn't have many facial cues—no visible mouth or eyes—I can convey a lot about what he's thinking by giving him a funny hat.

I'VE DECIDED TO BECOME A POP PSYCHOLOGIST. I NEED YOUR HELP TO MAKE MY LECTURE VIDEO.

YOU CAME TO THE RIGHT PLACE, BABE. FIRST, YOU NEED A NEW LOOK.

NICE TRY, BUT FRANKLY, THIS LOOK DIDN'T WORK TOO WELL FOR MADONNA EITHER.

© 1991 United Feature Syndicate, Inc.

7-30

NOSTRADOGBERT PREDICTS THERE WILL BE TURMOIL IN THE MIDDLE EAST.

WOW! THAT'S QUITE A PREDICTION! YOU'RE REALLY GOING OUT ON A LIMB!

© 1991 United Feature Syndicate, Inc.

IS THAT SARCASM? I CAN'T TELL WITH YOU.

WILL THERE BE ANY SAND INVOLVED?

12-11

The top of Dogbert's head is hard to draw. So I like hiding it with hats. **241**

WHAT DID YOU DO TO YOUR HAIR?

IT'S FOR MY NEW TELEVISION SHOW, "HEALING FOR DOLLARS." PEOPLE SEND MORE MONEY IF YOU HAVE THIS KIND OF HAIR.

6-15

IT MIGHT BE A TRICK.

THAT'S WHAT I THOUGHT UNTIL I SAW HIS HAIR.

CHECKS OR MONEY ORDERS

It's true!

WHY SHOULD I OPEN IT? YOU ALREADY TOLD ME IT'S JUST A STUPID HAT.

OPEN IT ANYWAY.

12-25

HEY, IT'S NOT REALLY A HAT; IT'S A CROWN.

I'M NOT HAPPY. I'M ONLY HUMORING YOU.

MERRY CHRISTMAS, LITTLE FRIEND.

I DECLARE MYSELF THE PATRON SAINT OF TECHNOLOGY.

1-31

I HEAL BROKEN TECHNOLOGY WITH MY RIGHT PAW AND I USE THE SCEPTER TO DRIVE OUT THE DEMONS OF STUPIDITY.

I DON'T THINK I'VE SEEN YOUR SPIRITUAL SIDE BEFORE.

OUT! OUT!

This hat design comes from a fancy folded napkin.

HOLD STILL WHILE I EXORCISE THE DEMONS OF STUPIDITY THAT POSSESS YOU.

OUT! OUT! I COMMAND YOU DEMONS OF STUPIDITY TO BE GONE!!

© 1994 United Feature Syndicate, Inc.

THE SUIT IS NOW SAFE.

THANKS!

I AM SAINT DOGBERT. I HAVE COME TO DRIVE OUT THE STALE AND OVERUSED JOKES ABOUT THE INFORMATION SUPER-HIGHWAY.

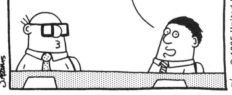

SOMETIMES I FEEL LIKE ROADKILL ON THE INFORMATION SUPERHIGHWAY!

© 1995 United Feature Syndicate, Inc. (NYC)

DON'T MAKE ME COME OVER THERE!

How many times have you heard that one?

MISTER DOGBERT, WE'VE DECIDED TO SEND YOU BACK TO EARTH AS AN ANGEL.

YOUR MISSION IS TO HELP PEOPLE IN NEED. WE HAVE GIVEN YOU SPECIAL POWERS.

WE'LL BE WATCHING.

© 1995 United Feature Syndicate, Inc. (NYC)

OKAY, SO WHAT'S THE PRICE FOR NEW HAIR PLUS BUNS OF STEEL?

AHEM

IT'S ALL ON THE PRICE SHEET.

This was based on a co-worker whose wife made his business suits.

The little dot-shading in Ted's hair is a pain, so now I just ink it black.

This is the most common "generic guy" I draw.

Ted the Generic Guy

Maybe you've noticed, but I don't have a wide artistic range. So when I need a new character to play a bit part, it often ends up looking like the same guy. Privately I call him "Ted, the generic guy," even though he sometimes has other aliases in the cartoon. Here are the many faces of Ted.

Ted started to be a regular but the other characters were more interesting.

DILBERT

By Scott Adams

DILBERT, I'D LIKE YOU TO INTRODUCE THE NEW GUY TO EVERYBODY.

GROAN

THIS WAY I NEVER HAVE TO LEARN THEIR NAMES.

THE FIRST STOP ON OUR ODYSSEY IS BUD.

UH... BUD, THIS IS THE NEW GUY, AND VICE-VERSA.

WHAT'S THIS?! ANOTHER PINK-BOTTOMED, IVY LEAGUE, MANAGEMENT "TRAINEE"?!

NEWS

IN MY DAY, YOU HAD TO START AT THE BOTTOM... AND BY GOLLY, YOU STAYED THERE!!

HOW LONG HAVE YOU WORKED HERE?

5-19

A WEEK... THIS HAPPENS PRETTY QUICKLY.

I met a "Bud" on my first day of work.

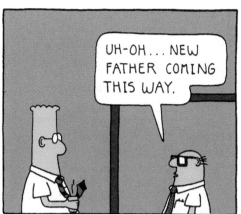

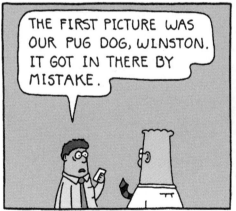

Could we all just agree that babies are ugly and leave it at that?

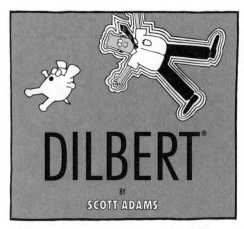

If I have to fire or kill someone, it's often the generic guy.

LOOK, TED! WE GET PAID THE SAME AS YOU BUT ALL WE'RE DOING IS STANDING AROUND AND FLICKING OUR FINGERS.

COME JOIN US AND FLICK YOUR FINGERS IN JOYOUS CELEBRATION THAT OUR PERFORMANCE IS NOT LINKED TO OUR PAY.

FLICK FLICK

I DON'T KNOW WHAT SUCCESS SOUNDS LIKE, BUT I'LL BET THIS ISN'T IT.

FLICK FLICK FLICK FLICK FLICK

← often he gets no lines.

I DON'T KNOW WHAT KIND OF GIFT TO BUY FOR TED'S BABY SHOWER.

HAND-CRAFTED ITEMS ARE GOOD. CUT THREE HOLES IN A PAPER BAG AND YOU'VE GOT A LOVELY BABY DRESS.

HE MIGHT THINK I'M CHEAP.

DO YOU THINK THE KID HAS A SALT SHAKER YET?

TED'S BABY SHOWER

OH LOOK, IT'S A STAPLER...

I CAN USE THIS TO TAKE UP THE HEM ON THE LOVELY HAND-CRAFTED PAPER BAG DRESS THAT DILBERT MADE.

IT LOOKS JUST LIKE THE ONE THAT DISAPPEARED FROM MY CUBICLE THIS MORNING.

EXCEPT YOURS HAD STAPLES.

sometimes Ted has dot eyes instead of ⊙⊙ eyes.

It's not good to think about these things.

Only jelly donuts make the "sploit" noise.

Slapstick Strips

Slapstick Strips One of the advantages of comics is that people who deserve a slap or a wedgie can get one. But it has to be carefully done to avoid complaints. For example, it's funny when a dog smacks a person, but I could never get away with having a person smack a dog—that would be cruel.

Here's a selection of my favorite slapstick strips, proving once again that violence can be funny.

I think you could get people hooked on exploding cigars if you marketed them well.

DILBERT® By Scott Adams

BE CANDID, DILBERT. WE HAVE A CORPORATE PHILOSOPHY THAT SAYS WE "DON'T SHOOT THE MESSENGER."

GOOD.

HAD YOU CONSULTED WITH THE ENGINEERING DEPARTMENT, YOU NEVER WOULD HAVE LAUNCHED SUCH AN ILL-CONCEIVED PRODUCT.

IT IS DOOMED TO FAIL. YOU WILL ALL BE HUMILIATED AND PROBABLY FIRED.

CAN'T I JUST WING HIM?!!

NO, EILEEN, THAT'S NOT OUR PHILOSOPHY.

IT TURNS OUT THE CORPORATE PHILOSOPHY IS A VERY FLEXIBLE DOCUMENT.

YOU'RE GETTING TAR ON THE CARPET.

Dilbert got tarred and feathered, in case it's hard to tell.

252

wouldn't this be fun?

Morale is a two-way street.

SHOULD RATBERT BE SPARED? SEND YOUR VOTE BY E-MAIL TO: SCOTTADAMS@AOL.COM

Don't send your vote. He was spared.

THE E-MAIL VOTES HAVE BEEN TABULATED. THE WILL OF THE PEOPLE IS THAT RATBERT SHALL BE SPARED FROM GETTING WHACKED WITH A MAGAZINE.

57% = SPARED

I GUESS THERE'S NOTHING FUNNY ABOUT RANDOM CRUELTY.

AAAII!!

RIGHT! CRUELTY IS ONLY FUNNY IF ADMINISTERED IN A PROPER SOCIAL CONTEXT.

11-29

I'M SORRY DAVE, BUT YOU'RE BEING TRANSFERRED TO MARKETING AND THERE'S NO BUDGET TO TRAIN YOU AS A MARKETER.

SLAP!

1-3-94

WHERE AM I? I NEED A DRINK.

THIS IS A TEMPORARY FIX... BUT YOU'LL FIT IN NOW.

I was in a bad mood when I drew this.

I MAY NOT BE SMART AND I MAY NOT BE ATTRACTIVE...

7-19

BUT I AM AERODYNAMIC!!

THAT MIGHT COME IN HANDY IN A MINUTE.

BLOW ON ME.

It sounds naughty, but it isn't.

I INVITED SAINT DOGBERT TO BLUDGEON ANYBODY WHO STRAYS FROM THE AGENDA INTO SOMETHING STUPID.

THAT REMINDS ME OF THE PRODUCTIZATION OF OUR TIGER TEAM'S PRIORITY MATRIX.

ACTUALLY, THAT WAS ON THE AGENDA.

OOPS. CARRY ON.

Dog hits man is funny, but not the other way around.

I'VE DECIDED TO MANAGE BY PHYSICAL INTIMIDATION. IF SOMEBODY SAYS SOMETHING STUPID I'LL JUST SMACK THEM.

THAT'S THE STUPIDEST THING I'VE EVER HEARD.

ON THE OTHER HAND, MAYBE I SHOULD GIVE IT A CHANCE.

SMACK!